T0199142

Hello,
My Name Is
RESILIENT

JESSICA SAGE

WESTBOW
PRESS®
A DIVISION OF THOMAS NELSON
& ZONDERVAN

WestBow Press books may be ordered through booksellers or by contacting:

WestBow Press
A Division of Thomas Nelson & Zondervan
1663 Liberty Drive
Bloomington, IN 47403
www.westbowpress.com
1 (866) 928-1240

ISBN: 978-1-9736-3830-8 (sc)
ISBN: 978-1-9736-3832-2 (hc)
ISBN: 978-1-9736-3831-5 (e)

Library of Congress Control Number: 2018910189

Print information available on the last page.

WestBow Press rev. date: 9/13/2018

"My entire life can be described in one sentence:
it didn't go as planned, and that's okay."
—Unknown

"Alternate sentence: you honestly can't make this stuff up."
—Me

"You don't understand now what I am doing,
but someday you will" (John 13:7 NLT).
—Jesus

To my kids: Rose, Etalemaw, Mishel,
Kevin, Gerson, and Jose Enrique.
Thank you for teaching me what really matters.

Contents

Part 3: Resilience in the Turbulence

Introduction
Beauty in the Brokenness

Today my brother and I said "we do" under a whitewashed gazebo as we gave away our mom's hand in marriage. Gathered around by Starbucks-sipping friends and family as witnesses, a man and woman promised to love and cherish each other for as long as they both shall live.

Needless to say, it was not your typical ceremony. The whole shebang was a re-creation of their first date that occurred exactly one year ago today. Having initially met via a popular online dating service, they had agreed to meet in person for the first time at our local Starbucks. They hit it off right away and spent hours talking and walking around the neighboring park.

One year later, they met again at that same Starbucks. This time, she was wearing a white dress and heels, and he was dressed to the nines in a silver tuxedo. Dozens of friends and family were there as well. Altogether, with coffee in hand, the wedding procession laced around the coffee shop and across the street to the park.

Horns blasted. Bystanders hollered. Cameras flashed.

The intimate ceremony was short, but the vows were eternal. And in one simple phrase, "I now pronounce you husband and wife," two families were blended into one.

I like to joke that my brother and I officially have "the whole set" now. We have a mom and a dad, a stepmom and a stepdad, a half-sister and a stepbrother. Our life is weird; it just is. I spend too many fear-filled nights too paralyzed by stress to be able to sleep. What is life going to be like now? So much is about to change.

You are being replaced, the devil whispers. *You are worthless. You are not good at anything*, he hisses. *The combination of a new family and the addition of more responsibility at work is too much for you.*

I toss and turn and think about why life is so hard. I foolishly let the devil's promptings become my truths.

No one could possibly understand how I am feeling.

I will never have a "normal" life.

I am unwanted.

I am all alone.

It is during these sleepless nights that God cups my face and calms my heart. He breathes His precious promises into my inner most being. "For I know the plans I have for you," says the Eternal, "plans for peace, not evil, to give you a future and hope—*never forget that*" (Jeremiah 29:11 The Voice).

He gently reminds me that I am not perfect, but He is. I can rest comforted by the fact that in my imperfection, in my loneliness, in my brokenness, He is good.

Japanese pottery has a centuries old reparation tradition called *kintsukuroi*, which translates to "golden repair." When an object is broken, the shattered pieces are mended back together with a lacquer containing flecks of gold or silver. Instead of tossing out the mess, the Japanese delicately piece it back together and practice the philosophy of *wabi-sabi*, understanding that the object is more beautiful for having been broken. It is said that the tradition originally stems from the concept of *mushin*, meaning the acceptance of change.

Change is so hard. It is easy to crave and give in to routine. Days would be so much easier if we only needed to wake up each morning and show up to school or work, where we could slowly snake around exerting as little effort as possible and avoiding confrontation before escaping back to the comfort of our homes.

Technology has aided this process, enabling us to skip even the short conversations of ordering food at restaurants and calling customer service agents for assistance. Now we can download "Skip the Line" apps and ask Siri for help.

But as attractive as that lifestyle may seem, it is equally as dangerous of a trap to fall into. It may be a comfortable way of living for you; but for me, when I allow that to become my routine for too long, I begin to crave purpose. I miss relationships. I lose sight of why I am here.

Because I am not alive merely to live comfortably. I cannot be surprised that my life is not "normal." I live to learn more about my Creator and to tell others about His unending goodness and grace that He continually floods into my life.

It is not easy, and I am not good at it. Along the way, I have fumbled. I have publicly dropped the ball and then stormed off the field to throw pity parties for myself. It happens over and over again, and it is not pretty. But God uses every fumble, every fall, and every misfortune to lead me to become resilient; He helps me recover from and adjust to change, to thrive amid adversity.

Ziad K. Abdelnour said that "there's no need to be perfect to inspire others. Let people get inspired by how you deal with your imperfections." But I must constantly remind myself that I am not designed to dwell in others' inspiration. It is not my goal to collect the attention, to rack up followers and likes, to earn power and respect. Instead of being driven by inspiration, it is my proud duty to reflect it. I am like the moon, gracefully reflecting the light of the Son to those who are lost and wandering through the dark.

This book is my story.

I do not write to impress you.

I do not write to entertain you.

I am here to tell you about my God, who turned my brokenness into His beauty.

Amen?

Amen.

I welcome you to enjoy the journey. Learn from my mistakes, glean from the lessons, and celebrate God's blessings. Jon Acuff said that "the scars you share become lighthouses for other people who are headed down the same rocks you hit." Just like Tyler Durden in *Fight Club*, "I don't wanna die without any scars." I pray that my story will be able to help you and inspire you to share your story with someone else. Let us learn and grow together.

Cheers!
Jessica Sage

Part 1

Resilience Amid the Circumstances

1

Once Upon a Time at Taco Bell
Resilience amid family circumstances

My story begins with my biological parents. The scene is set at a Taco Bell in the San Francisco Bay Area. My dad was the manager. He had begun working after his family moved to the United States from the Philippines, and quickly he maneuvered his way up into management. My mom worked there part time as a high school student. They fell in love and married young. Nine months later I arrived on the scene with cheeks as round and rosy as peaches and long, black locks that would make a young Kit Harington jealous.

As a little girl, I loved fairy tales and princesses; I bought into the Disney dream world of "once upon a times" and "happily ever afters." It was easy to do being spoiled. No one ever wants to admit that they were, but as a child, I can surely say I was spoiled.

In the awards ceremony of early life, I won first place in many categories and was rewarded with much attention. I was the first born to my young parents, and by default I was cast as both the experimental group and the control group in their parenthood project. Every parent wishes that there was a manual or remote or return slip for their precious children, but it is the role of the firstborn to make this adventure easier for the future siblings. (By the way, precious is the perfect adjective to describe children, as it can mean anything from adored and beloved, to expensive and priceless, to extremely sophisticated and picky! It can't get more appropriate than that.)

I also won first place prizes in being the first born in America within my dad's family and the first born in my generation throughout both my parents' families. This resulted in me being checked in and out of my home like a library book by my aunts and uncles, who were stricken with the baby fever.

I don't remember anything from my baby days, obviously, but I do know that I got around a lot. As an adult, I meet random people at parties and at the grocery store all the time who supposedly knew me as a baby. My long, dark, curly hair is now short, light, and straight with the help of periodic trims and boxed hair dye, but my round, rosy, peach cheeks are unmistakable.

"Do you remember me? Of course not. But when you were just this high," the stranger's voice will raise as his body lowers toward the floor, "you used to let me hold you." Then he will proceed to inform me of embarrassing stories involving me releasing some sort of bodily fluid onto his shirt. I just love meeting my parents' old friends, said no one ever.

Being your stereotypical Asian, I was obsessed with Hello Kitty as a little girl. Whenever I was interrogated by adults as to what my favorite color, favorite animal, and favorite place in the whole wide world was, I would promptly inform them blue, dolphins, and the Hello Kitty store at the mall. Thus, it was no surprise when I requested that my fifth birthday be Hello Kitty themed.

By this time, the baby fever had spread, and I had welcomed several younger cousins and my very own baby brother to the world. We had grown to become as thick as thieves, and obviously I wanted them all to attend my birthday party. When my mom announced that my Hello Kitty birthday party was to be at my cousin's house, I could not have thought of a grander plan.

I cannot recall the decorations or the games or the gifts from that party, but I do remember that I was thrilled to be with my favorite people. In the afternoon we had nap time, and at this early stage in life, we were fine with that. All quality, childhood, fun-filled days required times of recuperation to either get some shut-eye or quietly flip through picture books. On this particular day though, I remember my mom tiptoeing in and motioning for me to put my shoes on because we were about to go outside. Elated that I got to skip out on nap time, I leaped over my sleeping cousins.

Walks were another element of a quality, childhood, fun-filled day. (I now realize that taking care of children is like taking care of a dog: you make sure they get a walk, take a nap, have food and water, and have regularly scheduled potty times.) My mom and I strolled through the neighborhood hand in hand until after a short time she sat me down on the curb. The conversation we were about to have would be the turning point of my entire childhood.

While we were Hello Kitty party-ing it up at my cousin's house, my dad was at our own home packing. My mom explained that he was going to be staying at a different house with a different woman. I did not quite get it, but I nodded and skipped back to my party.

Once I fully understood what was happening, it hit me hard in the nighttime. Darkness would prompt me to swing open my door of imagination and let wondering and possible reasoning prance out and keep me company. *Where is Dad? Does he not love me anymore? What about "happily ever after"? Why is Mom crying? Why am I crying?* This tragedy marked the beginning of my battle with insomnia. Nights were haunted with endless questions and incessant tears. It carried on for months until one night my mom came into my room to calm my sobs with a different approach than she had used the countless nights before. This time she came equipped with a cure.

Moms are our own personal superheroes. Do you have a cold? She will come swooping in with some hot soup and crackers. Did you fall and scrape your knee? Here she comes, dashing in with Neosporin and Band-Aids. Did you have a bad day? Her arms are already spread wide open for an embrace. Did you get your heart broken? This one is a little bit more difficult, especially when Mom's heart is broken, too. Broken hearts are easy to console, but hard to cure. Superhero Mom came flying in anyway, cape flowing behind her, and I later realized that she did not fly in alone.

"Do you know why it hurts so much?" She pulled back the dark hair that was tear-glued to my cheeks. "It's because your heart is a puzzle, and right now a piece is missing." This line forever echoes in my soul.

When I was younger, I adored puzzles. First, it was those big wooden puzzles that you find in preschools with only five animal-shaped pieces. Then I graduated to alphabet floor puzzles, and soon I was able to move on to one-hundred- and two-hundred-piece beach scenes, floral arrangements, and replicas of famous painted masterpieces. Nothing is more frustrating than spending the time connecting edge pieces and matching color tones in middle areas, only to find that the last piece of your puzzle is missing.

"When your dad left, he took that last piece, hon." My eyes widened as she went on. "The only person who can fill that empty space is Jesus."

I had heard of Jesus before, as I had grown up going to church and had recently started kindergarten at the Christian school on the church property. If this Jesus wanted to fill the vacancy in my heart, then I would let Him. So my mom took my hands, and together we asked Jesus to be my missing puzzle piece.

The date was April 13, 2001. It became my second birthday, a good kind of birthday.

Verse for Thought

> "For God so loved the world, that he gave his only Son, that whoever believes in him should not perish but have eternal life." (John 3:16 ESV)

Reflection Questions

Mark Twain once said that "the two most important days in your life are the day you are born and the day you find out why." Do you have a second birthday? If so, when is it?

If you do not have one yet, dear friend, pray about it. Today can be your second birthday. The Bible says that "if you declare with your mouth that Jesus is Lord, and believe in your heart that God raised him from the dead, you will be saved" (Romans 10:9 ISV). If you would like to make that decision, read the following prayer aloud:

Let Us Pray

Jesus, be my everything.
I am broken; I have done wrong, and I am sorry.
Make me whole.
I believe that You are God, You are good, and You died to save me.
Thank You, Lord Jesus.
Through Your resurrection, I am made new.
Amen.

2

The Footloose of High School Musicals

Resilience amid lifestyle circumstances

I had grand expectations for high school. After all, I was beginning it right after the completion of the *High School Musical* trilogy. I couldn't wait for the carefree dancing, an effortless intelligence, and the handsome Zac Efron waiting for me in the welcome package. Boy, was I in for a surprise.

For starters, dancing was for sure a no-go. My private Christian school taught us that dancing makes babies. Yes, you read that right.

Dancing. Equals. Babies.

Needless to say, we did not have prom. Instead we had banquets where everyone stood around staring at one another until dinner, when everyone switched positions to *sitting* around staring at one another. It was quite the party.

About 99 percent of the alumni and roughly 100 percent of the current attendees at that high school will tell you that they hate it there. To be engulfed in such a structured community is difficult, especially for an adolescent. But to be honest, the lessons and truths that I gleamed during those painful years are priceless.

The school is named after the group of people in biblical times who lived in the ancient city of Berea, now modern-day Veria in Macedonia, Greece. (It always made me giggle when the office ladies would refer to us over the intercom as "Bereanites." It would be like calling people from Korea the "Koreanites.") The Bereans are only briefly mentioned in the book of Acts:

> The Jewish people here were more receptive than they had been in Thessalonica. They warmly and enthusiastically welcomed the message and then, day by day, would check for themselves to see if what they heard *from Paul and Silas* was truly in harmony with the Hebrew Scriptures. (Acts 17:11 The Voice)

Likewise, the faculty and staff encouraged us to be open-minded in our learning and to continually test our knowledge for ourselves. This process of thinking prepared me for the many challenges that were to come my way.

In life, I have learned that tests are not just multiple-choice questions and short-answer exams. It is more than sloppily filling in bubbles on scantrons and scribbling mumbo jumbo in giant letters across a blue book. Not all tests can be studied for (or "studied for" rather … *cough, cough*) and completed in one hour.

In life, most tests come unannounced. They come when we are unsuspecting and especially least ready. They wring us up and expose the ugliest parts of us, the parts that we thought were locked away in the closet with the key tossed. Then they leave us high and dry, eager to see how we will react in our naked and vulnerable state.

I received a lot of these pop tests during my high school career. Freshman year began with typical high school struggles: acne, friendship drama, and braces. I needed surgery to remove four adult teeth to relieve the extreme overcrowding in my tiny mouth. After surgery, I broke the fifth metatarsal in my foot while walking down the gymnasium bleachers. My awkward adolescent body was a mess!

After dealing with the physical trials, the emotional ones came rolling in. One of my aunts was diagnosed with cancer. Another aunt lost control of her addictions and was in a terrible car accident. Then my grandfather passed away. The culmination of these events led to my mother's diagnosis of post-traumatic stress disorder and gastroesophageal reflux disease.

My attention was being pulled in a million different directions, and I began to lose sight of myself. Being a people pleaser, I was striving to be there for everyone in their times of need. I wanted to be present, to be enough. Being a perfectionist, I was striving to get straight A's, to be enough. I wanted to do everything right, to be enough.

But "enough" is the threatening thirst in the desert of despair that cannot be quenched. I cannot be enough.

I will never be perfect.

The pursuit for perfection is my greatest struggle, my wayward focus, my biggest sin. But all the while, Jesus tugs at my heart and begs for my attention.

I will be enough.

I am perfect.

So calm your heart because I am holding it. Take courage because I am your strength. You need not strive unnecessarily because I am the way. Do not worry because I am truth. Fear not because I am life.

The next time you find yourself stranded in the desert futilely chasing after enough-ness, turn to the One who "transforms a *dry, lonely* desert into pools of *living* water, parched ground into lively springs" (Psalm 107:35 The Voice). The enemy is going to try to prolong your stay in the desert by reminding you of past transgressions, of the lack of notifications on your phone screen, of the absences of all those who used to always have your back.

Instead, run steadfastly to the One who will lead you beside still waters (Psalm 23:2b ESV).

When the summer break of '12 arrived, my dad bought my brother and me plane tickets to go visit him in Ohio. Little did we know that he really just needed a babysitter. One night he came into the room that my brother and I were sharing and began reprimanding us for our faith. He said it was ruining our lives because we were wasting our time with church, living for God, and surrendering our futures to Him. Instead, he believed we should have been prioritizing our future to achieve success.

In his mind, he had an equation drawn out for us:

Good grades
+ Good college
+ Good job
+ Good car
+ Good house
——————
= Success ($)

He meant if for our good. He wanted us to succeed and to be happy. What he didn't understand was that our faith is our measure of success and is the sole thing from which our happiness springs. I love the way that Eugene H. Peterson phrases it:

> But what happens when we live God's way? He
> brings gifts into our lives, much the same way that
> fruits appear in an orchard—things like affection
> for others, exuberance about life, serenity. We
> develop a willingness to stick with things, a sense
> of compassion in the heart, and a conviction that
> a basic holiness permeates things and people. We
> find ourselves involved in loyal commitments not
> needing to force our way into life, able to marshal

and direct our energies wisely. (Galatians 5:22–23 MSG)

I barely earned the gold cords at my high school graduation. I did not go to an Ivy League. I am not a doctor. I do not drive a Lambo' or a Ferrari. I still live with my mom. But I am happy. I have declared God's name on several continents. Dear friend, your worth is not defined by your grades, by your career, by your relationship status on Facebook, by your amount of Instagram followers, by your yoga pant size, or by the number of zeros in your bank account balance. Your worth is found in Jesus.

Verses for Thought

> "But the fruit of the Spirit is love, joy, peace,
> patience, kindness, goodness, faithfulness,
> gentleness, self-control; against such things there
> is no law." (Galatians 5:22–23 ESV)

Reflection Questions

Which fruit do you struggle with?

Which fruit are you best at?

What do you consider to be your greatest accomplishment?

How do you credit it to God? If you don't, it is not too late; how
can you credit it to God today?

Let Us Pray

God, I long to live Your way.
Thank You for the gifts You so graciously provide.
Guide me to use them for Your glory.
Amen.

3

Piercings Saved Our Lives
Resilience amid church circumstances

I have seven piercings. Six are on my left ear, one is on my right. I am often asked about the reasoning behind the unevenness. For a while I told people that I had just thought it looked pretty. It was something that I had gotten done during a rebellious period in my life when vanity had been a priority. A few years ago, I discovered a different, more beautiful meaning, and now this is the story that I tell.

My favorite part of any concert is when the artist sings a slow song and everyone in the crowd whips out their smartphone to turn on the flashlight and wave it around. I tear up every time, just as I do whenever we have the candlelit service on Christmas Eve. I find it just as bright and beautiful and marvelous as looking up at the thousands of stars on a clear night. I simply adore the individuality-turned-unity of it all.

It reminds me of the creation story in Genesis:

God: Let there be light.

And light flashed into being. God saw that the light was *beautiful and* good, and He separated the light from the darkness. God named the light "day" and the darkness "night." Evening gave way to morning. That was day one. (Genesis 1:3–5 The Voice)

And that's how it went:

God spoke.
Boom, it appeared.
He threw a *Life Is Good* sticker on there.
Called it a day.

Over and over, for six days until the world as we know it was created. Then He rested. I want you to think of your own favorite moment that makes you tear up a little. Maybe it's the morning sunrise on your way to work. Or the old couple who hold hands as they walk around your neighborhood. Or the Grand Canyon (after all, the manly man Ron Swanson says that crying is only acceptable at funerals and at the Grand Canyon!). Spend a minute with your eyes closed just dwelling in your moment. *How could He not call this good?*

The greatest part of all is that God thinks of us the same way.

Even when we sin.

Even when we lie.

Even when we fail.

Even when we stop thinking of Him that way.

He still loves us and humbly tilts our heads back toward Him. He welcomes us in a loving embrace, reminding us of His tears spilt and His blood shed. We never have to doubt that we are loved because we are His children and *He calls us good.*

And His love demands to be reciprocated. His love cannot be restricted to a two-way relationship; it longs to be spread around the neighborhood, among the community, across borders, and into new territories. Jesus said, "'Love the Lord your God with all your passion and prayer and intelligence.' This is the most important, the first on any list. But there is a second to set alongside it: 'Love others as well as you love yourself.' These two commands are pegs; everything in God's Law and the Prophets hangs from them" (Matthew 22:37–40 MSG).

We are called to love all people. I am going to say it again because this is a hard one: we are called to love *all* people. Even the mean ones, the condescending ones, the lying ones, the cheating ones, the lazy ones, the smelly ones, the ignorant ones, the pushy ones. It may be your first instinct to reject their imperfection and ignore them, or it may be your first impulse to candidly attempt to convert them to your own mind-set, your own way of life. But Billy Graham sagely reminds us that "it is the holy spirit's job to convict, God's job to judge and my job to love."

Our acceptance of people need not be based on mutual agreement or the overlooking of imperfection and condemnation. It is built on the cross. Pastor Brian Houston of Hillsong Church acquiesces, "If God wanted to condemn the world, He would have sent a condemner. But He wanted to save the world, so He sent us a Savior … we cannot reduce people's whole lives into one sweeping, judgmental statement filled with condemnation."

This principle can be juxtaposed with the story of Thomas. Case in point, you probably only remember who he is when "doubting" is paired with his name. Never mind Thomas's admirable decision to leave behind his old life to follow Jesus for years in discipleship, miracles, and ministry. The dude doubted *once*, and yet he is forever criticized for the time that he wanted physical proof that Jesus—who he watched get crucified—was alive. Thomas had missed out on the first reunion between Jesus and His disciples.

When I was younger, I used to have the fear that I would miss out on things, so I would refuse to sleep during nap time. Because what if I missed out on something cool? What if the ice-cream man drove into the neighborhood? What if my friends came by to ask me out to play? What if Tupac came back?

Today, as we are encountering people and exuding love toward them, we should be fearing that we miss out on the opportunity to share our incredible message of salvation. This last spring, I had the privilege of attending a Hillsong United concert in the Roman Colosseum in Caesarea, Israel. These were the exact stones where Paul pleaded his case in a trial before King Agrippa. In true Paul fashion, his conversation quickly turned into his conversion story. In response, Agrippa tells Paul, "You almost persuade me to be a Christian" (Acts 26:28b MEV). May we live in fear of "almost."

Walt Disney said that "you can design and create, and build the most wonderful place in the world. But it takes people to make the dream a reality." People are essential. Fellowship is healthy. Community is necessary. We are to love all people, even the undeserving. This quote by Robert Murray McCheyne is scribbled inside the front cover of my Bible: "If you would be like Christ, give much, give often, give freely, to the vile and poor, the thankless and the undeserving. Christ is glorious and happy and so will you be."

The common misconception that "all Christians are perfect" is consequently paired with the reality that they are not, and both the non-Christians and Christians are left feeling confused and disappointed. Christians are not perfect. Christians are people.

The Church is not perfect, because the Church is not a building—it is the people. It is often said that "a church is not a museum for good people; it's a hospital for the broken." Some churches are led by individuals who are strict and conservative and political, and I am sorry if you have gotten hurt along the way. But you were not hurt by the Church, you were hurt by people. There is still a bigger, stronger, healthier network out there within the Church longing to be a beacon of hope and an estuary of grace for you.

So find a church body with your kind of people; a place where you feel at home. No one church is better than the rest. It's not a rivalry like among sports teams. Each church location is just another room in God's house. Salvation is not based on the style of music played, or whether communion is taken out of a communal loaf and wine cup, or out of fun little prepackaged cracker and juice combo cups. Church is simply a collective of people living life together by seeking to serve the magnificent Creator, *who calls us good.*

Verse for Thought

> "One day spent in your house, this beautiful place of worship, beats thousands spent on Greek island beaches. I'd rather scrub floors in the house of my God than be honored as a guest in the palace of sin." (Psalm 84:10 MSG)

Reflection Questions

How do you spend your Sundays?

What church do you go to, and how are you connected there?

If you don't go to one, find one near you and pay it a visit!

Let Us Pray

> *Oh, God,*
> *How amazing You are!*
> *I dedicate my time to You.*
> *You are the ultimate source of dedication and hope.*
> *Help me to pursue Your creation with everything in me.*
> *I do not want to miss a moment with You,*
> *Nor any moments where I can share Your love.*
> *Amen.*

4

Buckets

Resilience amid tempting circumstances

When my brother turned seventeen last spring, I promised him that I would take him on a trip to Europe later this fall. We have been planning for several months, and I have spent several thousands of dollars in booking charges already. (Yes, I proudly and ever so humbly accept the Best Sister of the Year Award.)

After browsing through countless travel blogs, informational pamphlets, and magazines, what we are looking forward to most is the food. My mouth waters just thinking about all the Belgian waffles, Swiss cheese, and French croissants that I am going to scarf down. But I have been warned by multiple informants that I should not get my hopes up too high, because often the taste and elements of international food become misconstrued within American cuisine.

We Americans tend to sugarcoat everything and then justify it to fit our "needs." I read a meme the other day that said "chocolate comes from cocoa, which is a tree. That makes it a plant. Therefore, chocolate counts as salad." Come on, people; this is why so many Americans are obese!

We buy popcorn at movie theaters, because it feels funny not to; as if we are missing out on something and fear not fitting in. Then we proceed to buy the extra-large bucket of popcorn, because it comes with a free refill. So as we roll away with our little red wagons spilling over with extra-buttered popcorn and soda pop, we feel great for having scored such a good deal.

At Christians, we need to be watchful as our enemy tries to sugarcoat our nearest and dearest temptations in life. Because temptations can come in so many ways, shapes, and forms, it can often be hard to identify them when they first appear. But just like in school when we were unsure of what was going to be on an upcoming, important exam, our teachers would issue us a warning: "If I say it out loud, it's going to be on the test." Likewise, Jesus forewarns us that there are struggles we will face, solutions to overcome them, and but He will be there every step of the way.

Jesus warned us clearly: "Beware indeed of those in a world filled with obstacles and temptations *that cause people to turn away from Me.* Those temptations are woven into the fabric of a world *not yet redeemed*, but beware to anyone who lures righteous women and men off the narrow path" (Matthew 18:7 The Voice).

Temptations turn our eyes away from God. They cut us off from our direct line to His goodness and grace that showers us with peace and happiness. Temptation will say and do anything to get you to trade all the fruit in the world for the one, shiny, bad apple. That is what makes temptations different from trials.

Trials are difficulties that collide with blessings in the beautifully juxtaposed roller-coaster of life that God rides *with* us. Our trials teach us, mold us, and stretch us to grow into our full heavenly potential. Meanwhile, temptations require a choice. C. S. Lewis warns that, "you will certainly carry out God's purpose, however you act, but it makes a difference to you whether you serve like Judas or like John."

When I visited Israel, my tour guide told us that shopping is temptation from the devil! "Seriously, though, guys," he would say as we bypassed all of the "forbidden" gift shops. "I am saving you money."

One-click-away technology is making everything so accessible these days. Oh, how many times I have succumbed to the lies that the enemy has whispered in my ear. "Can you imagine how many likes on Instagram you will receive if you buy and wear this outfit?" He points to the trendy things in your cart. "But you *need* those shoes to fit in!" Loss of control over finances, over tempers, and over addictions to food or substances can become serious problems and distractions from our faith.

Paul wrote that "those who chase riches are constantly falling into temptation and snares. They are regularly caught by their own stupid and harmful desires, dragged down and pulled under into ruin and destruction" (1 Timothy 6:9 The Voice). So how do we keep our heads above the waves?

James asked the same question to get to the root of the problem:

> What causes fights and quarrels among you? Don't they come from your desires that battle within you? You desire but do not have, so you kill. You covet but you cannot get what you want, so you quarrel and fight. You do not have because you do not ask God. When you ask, you do not receive, because you ask with wrong motives, that you may spend what you get on your pleasures. You adulterous people, don't you know that friendship with the world means enmity against God? Therefore, anyone who chooses to be a friend of the world becomes an enemy of God. (James 4:1–4 NIV)

Bottom line, it is a heart issue. If our hearts' greatest desire is to embody money, power, or respect, then we are going to end up exhausted from endless circling, like a dog chasing its tail. "Don't hoard treasure down here where it gets eaten by moths and corroded by rust—or worse!—stolen by burglars. Stockpile treasure in heaven, where it's safe from moth and rust and burglars. It's obvious, isn't it? The place where your treasure is, is the place you will most want to be, and end up being" (Matthew 6:19–21 MSG).

My family started attending the new Hillsong Church extension in San Francisco a few months ago. The first worship service that we attended was led by Ben Houston, pastor of Hillsong Los Angeles and son of the Australian church founders Pastors Brian and Bobbi Houston. His sermon, entitled "The Show Must Go On," beautifully pointed out the dangerous flaw in our tendency to live out our Christian faith by the same popular show-business standard.

When circumstances arise, it can become so easy to get swept into the grind and merely go through the motions. "After all, the show must go on," we reason. Ironically, one of the spotlights on stage caught on fire midsermon. Amid the chaos and screaming, Ben was able to remain calm and continue on as volunteers extinguished the fire.

He gently reminded us that when people approach us with their struggles and their anguish, it can be so easy to brush them aside so that we can tackle our own difficulties. Distracting thoughts can barrage our minds: "Life is tough, and there is not enough time."

But hold on! Jesus died for you. He died for me. He died for people. He called us to love all people, remember?

Sometimes, I hate the GPS on my phone. The first thing I do when I climb into my car every day is set up the directions to guide me to work. I do not do that because I still do not know how to get to work (although that is sometimes debatable); I do it in case there is an accident up ahead, and I can calculate how long it will take me to get to work.

Oftentimes I will make pit stops to fill up on gas or grab a quick latte from Starbucks. When I do, Siri gets mad. She will start yelling, "Make a U-turn up ahead. Make a U-turn up ahead. Make a U-turn up ahead." And I counter back with, "Stop it, Siri!

It's okay! I know where I am going!" (It's a very mature process, I assure you).

My favorite comedian, Tim Hawkins, does a bit about how he wishes there was a GPS for relationships because "guys don't know!" He then acts out a hilarious dialogue between himself and his imaginary GPS about an interaction with his wife:

GPS: say something about her hair.

Tim: Hey … what's up with your hair?!?!

* Pause *

GPS: … recomputing.

The great thing is that we have the living, breathing Word of God to act as our life GPS. When difficulties come our way, we can open our Bibles and recalibrate our hearts with truth and hope. We can learn from the characters in the Bible like Job and David and Joseph, who all suffered so much both physically and emotionally. But when they were in the middle of it all and did not see why they were suffering, they sought out God, and that was enough.

If our hearts' greatest desire is to avoid pain to seek perfection, then we are going to be disappointed. Our pain and imperfection are part of the process. Jesus's disciples learned this the hard way when Jesus revealed to them the agenda of His death and resurrection. Peter thought he knew best, as we so often think that we know best.

"If only we can skip the torture and enter into paradise together, all will be well."

But instead Jesus answered, "Get behind Me, you tempter! You're thinking only of human things, not of the things God has planned" (Mark 8:33 The Voice).

Our perfection can only be found through Jesus's pain. It is not fair, but on our own we fail. So love came down and conquered all. Now we are called to go—connect with God's people. Go, tell it on the mountains, that Jesus Christ was born; then died; but rose again. Simply believe in the ultimate, beautiful love story, and you shall be saved.

Verse for Thought

"Go out into the world and share the good news with all of creation." (Mark 16:15 The Voice)

Reflection Question

In what area of your life could you use a recalibration?

Let Us Pray

God,
Thank You for Your Son, for Your Sacrifice, for saving me.
Recalibrate my heart to Your truth.
When life seems hard and unfair,
I will dwell on Your goodness and Your grace, and I will go;
I will go share Your story of love and provision.
Amen.

5

Fast and Furious
Resilience amid still circumstances

We go through life so fast these days—perhaps I more than anyone. In high school I ran track and field; sprints and relays were my jam. As I ran, I would repeat my mantra in my head over and over again: *Be fast or be last! Be fast or be last!* I lived for the thrill of building momentum and passing others up.

When I learned how to drive, I translated that into my driving. I gained top speeds so that I could pass other cars. My mantra then changed to the first line in Disney Pixar's *Cars*, "Okay ... Here we go. Focus. Speed. I am speed."

Now, however, I have learned my lesson. Six hundred dollars' worth of speeding tickets will do that to you. I'm just kidding ... not really. I now drive in the slow lane and am running distance races. My first half marathon is in two weeks, and in this process, I had to adjust my training from the quick sprints to the painful, slow-but-steady-wins-the-race sort of pace.

It is hard to pace yourself. We are hardwired to want things right away. This is why we have On Demand TV, Uber Eats, and rumors of Amazon delivery drones. I was at Chick-fil-A the other day, and my order was ready before I even slid my card!

God could have easily created the world in one day. He could have snapped His fingers on day one and then hopped in His recliner to binge watch *Star Wars* for the rest of the week. I know that's what I would have done! But instead He decided to take all seven. He worked for six days and rested for one—He paced Himself.

Without a break, we allow our lifestyles to fall under the niche of numbness. We buy cushy shoes and lounge in cushy seats. My family recently watched a movie in one of those theaters where you can reserve a recliner. Good heavens, it was delightful! But we have dangerously allowed our lives to become so cushy for the sake of comfort. The idea of crossing over and out of our comfort zones has become terrifying.

I used to refuse to take the elevator. Instead, I would endure the perilous journey up and down the stairs. Even in the tall skyscrapers that shape the skyline of San Francisco, I would choose the independence of stairs. I wanted to set my own pace instead of trust the ability of the elevator.

Because, you see, elevators make annoying, unplanned stops. I am reminded of the scene in *Elf* when Buddy presses all the floor level buttons on the elevator when he joyfully realizes that when altogether pressed, the buttons illuminate in the shape of a festive Christmas tree. The other businessman in the elevator was not pleased when Buddy then exited, leaving him alone to stop at every level unnecessarily.

Elevators also rely on cables that carry the potential for stopping, snapping, and/or dropping you down to your death. Every time we drive past a particular hotel chain, my mom reminds us of the time that she and her sister were trapped in an elevator during a family Disneyland trip. They had selected the appropriate button, and the elevator swiftly carried them to our floor level—or *almost* our floor level. When the elevator came to a stop, the door could only slightly crack open enough to reveal that the elevator had stopped about a foot short of the hallway's ground level. The two girls giddily waited for technicians to break them free from their very own Tower of Terror ride.

Some people's perception of God may resemble something similar to an elevator. It may seem like God carries us to annoying, unplanned stops. It may seem like God lets us fall to the depths of despair. But He never abandons us. In contrast, He brings us *with* Him to resting spots to strengthen our reliance on Him.

> *Listen!* The Lord, the Eternal, the Holy One of Israel says,
>
> > Eternal One: In returning and rest, you will be saved. In quietness and trust you will find strength.
> >
> > *God invites His people to lean only on Him. If they will just stop their busyness and self-reliance, God will be able to take care of them.*
> >
> > But you refused. You couldn't sit still; instead, you said, "No! We will ride out of here on horseback. Fast horses will give us an edge in battle." But those who pursue you will be faster still. (Isaiah 30:15–16 The Voice)

Our spiritual journey will lose steam without stillness. Stillness restores the soul. It transforms small thinking. It activates the metamorphosis of our lives. Butterflies are only rewarded with maturity after persevering through a period of stillness.

When I visited Israel, I learned quite a bit about Jewish tradition regarding Shabbat. I had previously considered the observation of the Sabbath to be ritualistic and controlling. My rebellious nature instinctively painted a jaded view of the tradition. *How could anyone not do* anything *for a whole day?* I would argue.

But stillness is different from rest. It's not staying in bed binge watching *Grey's Anatomy* all day. Getting R & R at a five-star, all-inclusive resort on the sandy shores of Hawaii is not the same as stillness. The Lord commands us to "be still, be calm, see and understand I am the True God" (Psalm 46:10a The Voice).

We practice stillness when we meet difficulties and when we see desperation but choose to deny ourselves and instead direct our needs to God.

We can prepare by participating in stillness Sabbaths—just wasting time with God. Spending a day offline. Choosing to open the Bible instead of text bubbles. Engraving truths on our hearts for the tough times.

In church and in school, we used to repeatedly study the parable of the sower. It would drive me crazy reviewing the same story over and over again. It was not until my trip to Israel—when I heard Jesus's tale while walking along an actual dirt path and through a real vineyard—that the meaning began to sink in. As we climbed over rocks and stepped around weeds, the words seeped through to my heart.

> Jesus: Once a farmer went out to scatter seed *in his fields.* Some seeds fell along a trail where they were crushed underfoot by people walking by. Birds flew in and ate those seeds. Other seeds fell on gravel. Those seeds sprouted but soon withered, depleted of moisture *under the scorching sun.* Still other seeds landed among thorns where they grew for a while, but eventually the thorns stunted them so they couldn't thrive or bear fruit. But some seeds fell into good soil—*soft, moist, free from thorns.* These seeds not only grew, but they also produced *more seeds,* a hundred times what the farmer originally planted …

I want you to understand, so here's the interpretation: The voice of God falls on human hearts like seeds scattered across a field. Some people hear that message, but the devil opposes the liberation that would come to them by believing. So he swoops in and steals the message from their hard hearts like birds stealing the seeds from the footpath. Others receive the message enthusiastically, but their vitality is short-lived because the message cannot be deeply rooted in their shallow hearts. In the heat of temptation, their faith withers, like the seeds that sprouted in gravelly soil. A third group hears the message, but as time passes, the daily anxieties, the pursuit of wealth, and life's addicting delights outpace the growth of the message in their hearts. Even if the message blossoms and fruit begins to form, the fruit never fully matures because the thorns choke out the plants' vitality.

But some people hear the message and let it take root deeply in receptive hearts made fertile by honesty and goodness. With patient dependability, they bear good fruit. (Luke 8:5–8a, 10b–15 The Voice)

Stillness softens hearts, making them receptive, so that in the heat of temptation, we know to look to Him on whom we can depend. Because we still have a long way to go.

Verse for Thought

> "So since we stand surrounded by all those who
> have gone before, an enormous cloud of witnesses,
> let us drop every extra weight, every sin that clings
> to us and slackens our pace, and let us run with
> endurance the long race set before us." (Hebrews
> 12:1 The Voice)

Reflection Question

What is the extra weight that you need to drop?

Let Us Pray

> *Lord God,*
> *There is still a long way to go, and I am getting*
> *tired.*
> *I offer up this extra weight to You, God.*
> *Thank You for caring for me and for carrying my*
> *burdens.*
> *Help me to follow Your example and learn to be*
> *still this week.*
> *Amen.*

6

Less *13 Reasons Why*, More Psalm 13
Resilience amid depressing circumstances

I used to worry that I would not be able to withstand the perils of the distant journey. Why am I struggling here and now, when I could be in heaven where I can just happily worship my King twenty-four seven? I became depressed and suicidal. I would sit in the kitchen holding the biggest knife we had, knowing it could all be over with one cut. I would stand on the second story of the mall or at the balcony of hotels and imagine that in one leap I could be home. I just wanted to die.

Depression is serious. Suicidal thoughts are serious. But both are common occurrences in the Bible. It is less *13 Reasons Why* and more Psalm 13. The psalm was written by King David, the man after God's own heart. Despite being one of the most famous, godly leaders in the Bible, he still struggled with depression and despair. Yet, no one prescribed him Prozac. No one locked him up in an asylum. Instead, he prayed. David shared with God what was in his heart, and in just six simple verses, David's song morphs from one of agony to one of adoration:

O Lord, how long will you forget me? Forever?
How long will you look the other way?
How long must I struggle with anguish in my soul, with sorrow in my heart every day?
How long will my enemy have the upper hand?

Turn and answer me, O Lord my God!
Restore the sparkle to my eyes, or I will die.
Don't let my enemies gloat, saying, "We have
defeated him!"
Don't let them rejoice at my downfall.
But I trust in your unfailing love.
I will rejoice because you have rescued me.
I will sing to the Lord
because he is good to me.

In the heat of temptation, when I was at my lowest and had
nowhere else to look except for up, the Lord reminded me of His
presence and His promise to help: "I've told you all this so that
trusting me, you will be unshakable and assured, deeply at peace.
In this godless world you will continue to experience difficulties.
But take heart! I've conquered the world" (John 16:33 MSG).

Just like when Elijah said, "Lord, I want to die," God provided
him with the strength to live (see 1 Kings 19:4). Just when my
Hallelujah was tired, He provided me with a new song. God
deserves to be praised in the good times and praised in the hard
times. His process refines us, keeping us humble in success and
diligent in failure.

We are never left to fend for ourselves. "For no one is
abandoned by the Lord forever. Though he brings grief, he also
shows compassion because of the greatness of his unfailing love.
For he does not enjoy hurting people or causing them sorrow"
(Lamentations 3:31–33 NLT). In fact, "it is good to have to deal
with restraint and burdens when young" (Lamentations 3:27 The
Voice). Whether that means young in body, young in spirit, or
young in faith, "don't let anyone put you down because you're
young. Teach believers with your life: by word, by demeanor, by
love, by faith, by integrity" (1 Timothy 4:12 MSG). Jesus said that
"unless you return to square one and start over like children,
you're not even going to get a look at the kingdom, let alone get in.

Whoever becomes simple and elemental again … will rank high in God's kingdom" (Matthew 18:3–4 MSG).

I love watching the genuine look of surprise on children's faces on Christmas and the loving glances that they give their parents during cuddle sessions. That right there—the precious joy, the unconditional love, the unbreakable bond—is what God longs for. He gave up His own Son because He loved us just as much (see John 3:16). He left behind ninety-nine others because He wanted to personally bring another one home safe and sound (see Luke 15).

Sometimes good parents let bad things happen so that their children can learn and grow. A parent can warn a toddler not to touch a hot stovetop, but the child often will not truly learn until he finds out for himself and gets burned. It is then that the toddler understands that the parent was right, and that the parent was looking out for the toddler because of his undying love for him.

Rather than ridding us of bad things, God gives us the freedom to learn and grow for ourselves. But He is our good, good Father. He never leaves. He remains near with His arms outstretched to catch us when we fall and to hold us when we are down. I love the way that Christian hip-hop artist Lecrae puts it: "How can Christians be salt and light if they never encounter meat and darkness? You cannot stomp something you're running away from. You cannot influence something you never encounter."

Paul reminds us that "any temptation you face will be nothing new. But God is faithful, and He will not let you be tempted beyond what you can handle. But He always provides a way of escape so that you will be able to endure *and keep moving forward*" (1 Corinthians 10:13 The Voice).

When we abide, He provides.

Many celebrities and speakers receive daily allotments to carry them through the demands and necessities of daily living. In the same way, God gives us a daily portion. His provision is plenty; in fact, His provision is abundant. It is often said that "*what you give is what you get.* What you sow, you harvest" (Galatians 6:7b The Voice). But with God, the harvest is far more plentiful than what we sow.

The means and the timing, however, are not always what we would expect. God is prepared. He planted the sycamore tree long before Zaccheus longed to see Jesus (see Luke 19). But He reveals His provision only when He *knows* we are ready, not when we *think* we are. Even with His faithful disciples, Jesus kept testing and building their trust by keeping them on their toes.

> Disciples: *But we don't have enough food.* We only have five rounds *of flatbread* and two fish.
> Jesus: Bring the bread and the fish to Me. (Matthew 14:17–18a The Voice)

He knows we have little on our own. He wants us to *draw near* so that He can transform our little into more than enough. "*So the disciples brought Him the five rounds of flatbread and the two fish,* and Jesus told the people to sit down on the grass. He took the bread and the fish, He looked up to heaven, He gave thanks, and then He broke the bread. Jesus gave the bread to the disciples, and the disciples gave the bread to the people; everyone ate and was satisfied. *When everyone had eaten,* the disciples picked up 12 baskets of *crusts and* broken pieces *of bread and crumbs*" (Matthew 14:18b–20 The Voice).

God could have provided just enough. But time and time again He reveals Himself in moments of need with abundance. God shatters expectations and shows up with more than our anticipations.

He shut hungry lion mouths for Daniel.

He split the raging Red Sea for Moses.

He froze the blazing sun in the sky for Joshua.

He broke down prison gates for Peter.

He brought life to the barren womb for Sarah.

He denied the power of death for Lazarus.

He tore the veil for you and me.

He is just waiting for us to look to heaven. "Just ask and it will be given to you," He promises (Matthew 7:7a The Voice). "Come to Me, all who are weary and burdened, and I will give you rest" (Matthew 11:28 The Voice).

So go.

Drown in His presence.

Dance in His goodness.

Sing of His mercy.

Thank Him for His grace.

Drink in His blessings.

He is waiting.

13 Reasons Why Not

1. **You are loved.**

   "For God loved the world so much that he gave
   his only Son. God gave his Son so that whoever
   believes in him may not be lost, but have eternal
   life." (John 3:16 ICB)

2. **You are chosen.**

   "*Remember* you are people who have been set
   apart for Him; He has chosen you to be His own
   possession out of all the peoples on the earth."
   (Deuteronomy 14:2 The Voice)

3. **You have a future.**

   "'For I know the plans I have for you,' says the
   Eternal, 'plans for peace, not evil, to give you a
   future and hope—never forget that.'" (Jeremiah
   29:1 The Voice)

4. **You are not alone.**

   "Be strong. Take courage. Don't be intimidated.
   Don't give them a second thought because God,
   your God, is striding ahead of you. He's right
   there with you. He won't let you down; he won't
   leave you." (Deuteronomy 31:6 MSG)

5. **You are strong.**

   "I can do all things because Christ gives me the
   strength." (Philippians 4:13 NLV)

6. **You are provided for.**

   "My God will richly fill your every need in a glorious way through Christ Jesus." (Philippians 4:19 GW)

7. **You have a purpose.**

   "For we are God's masterpiece. He has created us anew in Christ Jesus, so we can do the good things he planned for us long ago." (Ephesians 2:10 NLT)

8. **You are comforted.**

   "He comforts us in all our trouble, so that we can then comfort people in every kind of trouble, through the comfort with which God comforts us." (2 Corinthians 1:4 NTE)

9. **You are cared for.**

   "Give your worries to the Lord, and he will take care of you. He will never let good people down." (Psalm 55:22 NCV)

10. **You have hope.**

    "May the God of hope fill you with all joy and peace in believing, so that by the power of the Holy Spirit you may abound in hope." (Romans 15:13 ESV)

11. **You are unique.**

    "I will offer You my grateful heart, for I am Your *unique* creation, filled with wonder and awe. You have approached even the smallest details with excellence; Your works are wonderful; I carry this knowledge deep within my soul." (Psalm 139:14 The Voice)

12. **You are remembered.**

"You keep track of all my sorrows. You have collected all my tears in your bottle. You have recorded each one in your book." (Psalm 56:8 NLT)

13. **You are forgiven.**

"But if we confess our sins, he is faithful and just to forgive us our sins and cleanse us from everything we've done wrong." (1 John 1:9 CEB)

Reflection Question

Who else in your life needs to hear those truths?

Let Us Pray

> *Lord,*
> *I come to You as I am.*
> *Thank You for Your acceptance, for Your love, for Your promises.*
> *You are so good, and You are on my side!*
> *This week, I choose to abide in You.*
> *Amen.*

PART 2

Resilience Because of Consequences

7

Let Go and Let God
Resilience because of consequences from uncertainty

"Alright, folks, we will be evacuating you from this aircraft as quickly as possible. Please gather your belongings; the cabin door will be opening momentarily."

My plane had not yet ascended. It should have been peaceably docked at the gate instead of being ferociously rocked back and forth like a ship about to be capsized by a strong, invincible wave.

I had taken the day off from work to finally begin the college visit tour that all my friends had completed five years prior. Community college had always been the unspoken plan, so I did not conduct the traditional junior year of high school scrutiny of universities with my peers.

Both of my parents had attended the same local junior college that I enrolled in and both expected me to earn an associate degree and then transfer. Yet there I was, half of a decade later, about to visit a school that sent me more-than-too-much junk mail overflowing with eager promises of guidance to easily obtain the degree I so zealously craved.

My hunger for a diploma was not driven by my thirst for knowledge. In fact, that couldn't be further from the truth. My reasoning was torn evenly fifty-fifty. Half of me wanted a degree just to have one; to be readily equipped for whatever career opportunities flew my way. I thought of it like a valuable lucky penny that I could tuck safely away in my wallet for a rainy day.

The other half of me wanted one to please my parents. Neither of them had graduated, let alone earned an associate degree; I was determined to do both.

One thing stood in my way: my stubbornness against the school system. My rebellion began in high school when I discovered my kinesthetic learning style. If I wasn't actively applying my knowledge in real-life situations, then how was I supposed to remember it? No adult I knew regularly quoted the *Iliad* and the *Odyssey* or used the Pythagorean theorem or recalled the events of the War of 1812 to make it through each day.

So I began boycotting essays and tests. I joined the student government to enact change in my school. My involvement with planning and hosting school events earned me time away from my desk, and I abused that privilege as much as possible. "Yeah, I won't be in class tomorrow. I need to set up for that thing ..."

In college I discovered that the teachers were not as concerned about attendance as my previous teachers were. In high school, if you were not in the classroom during attendance in third period because you stopped by the bathroom before class, the office would have already called your mom, grandfather, and neighbor's dog to investigate where you were.

At the community college, I quickly learned how to calculate just how many class sessions I needed to actually attend in order to still earn participation points. By just glancing at the syllabus, I could tell which assignments were vital and which I could easily skip and still pass the class. The first few weeks of the semester I would sit up front and ask multiple questions to establish my presence and demonstrate a fabricated intelligence. Then, I would disappear until the mandatory final exam. Obviously, my attitude did not get me far. My self-destruction left me high and dry with nothing but a transcript of alphabet soup.

So what do you want to do when you grow up then? That question robbed me of too many nights and recurrently sickened me to my core. Now, don't get me wrong. It's not that I had *no* idea what I wanted to do with my life. It's that I had way too many awesome ideas. This is the evolution of my career goal throughout my college years:

- Become a physical therapist

I had been paying for my tuition by working full time at a sporting goods store. A friend in one of my communications classes had informed me of what would become my favorite college class ever: Occupational Work Experience. This class allowed me to receive college credit for simply going to my job, which I loved! Finally, I had found a class where I was paid to show up.

All that was required of me was a short paper due at the end of the semester regarding goals formed and completed over the course of the class. The amount of credits received were directly related to the relevance of your career. If your job coincided with your major, then you received an extra unit each semester.

I quickly declared that my major was kinesiology, the study of body movement, to go with my sporting goods retail job. I spent three semesters taking only this class, which means I was physically on campus for a total of about fifteen minutes each of those semesters when I had to meet with my co-op counselor to turn in the goals paper (hint: copy, paste.).

My decision to pursue becoming a physical therapist was also due to the fact that at the time, my grandma (who is unbelievably awesome!) was seeing her own PT. She had hurt herself flying over the handlebars of her bike at the city skateboard park. (That's my grandma, yo. The original gangster.) I was able to use the knowledge that I had obtained in a sports med class to explain to her the reasoning behind her diagnosis and treatment plans due to different stages of inflammation and blah blah blah—I just felt ubersmart being able to use my little bit of knowledge in real-world situations. But then I failed anatomy twice and realized that I couldn't memorize squat, so that dream didn't last long.

- Become president

Of what? The United States, obviously. Go hard or go home, baby. "I did the math, and I can become president in 2036, so remember this face." That was my catchphrase. I changed my major to Political Science having taken exactly zero government classes and felt great. I did my own research, and my managers giggled as they passed by the break room and saw me reading my books on terrorism and generation differences on my lunch hours.

- Become a real-life Leslie Knope

Yes, I looked into majoring in Environmental Studies/ Recreation, Parks and Tourism Admin only because *Parks and Recreation* is the best show ever.

- Become a photojournalist/professional blogger/just-plain-famous Instagram-travel model.

I experimented with an unsuccessful travel blog. And with that, that short-lived dream was over.

- Become a teacher

Now this is an interesting one because of one simple fact: I hate kids. When I am out running errands and the kids in the aisle over start to fuss, I will leave my cart and dash out. When I am at work and children come inside to play with the various balls and bikes that we have on display, I will immediately take my break.

I think what makes me hate them so much is that they are ironically drawn to me like bugs to a lantern. One year we were on our annual family vacation to Disneyland and we had just gotten off the water ride. A little boy dodged his way through the crowd until he found his way to me and tugged on my wet shirtsleeve. "Lost!" he whined. Annoyed and amazed that out of all the teachers and caregivers in my family he had managed to find the one person who hated kids, I reluctantly reunited him with his worried family.

My decision to pursue teaching was mostly influenced by my family. Three generations on my mom's side have attended the same Christian school from kindergarten to eighth grade and then proceeded to work there later as adults. If you count my great-grandpa, who built the school's gymnasium, then I am the fourth generation to work there. My family makes up a large portion of the school board and staff, as well as the church that is associated with the school and meets in one of the classrooms on the weekends.

As a child, I would spend six or seven days a week at the school, often for twelve hours a day, even in the summer. Being the eldest sibling and cousin, I was always designated as the babysitter. My brother, younger cousins, and I helped some days by scrubbing toilets or painting walls, and other days we spent playing any and every sport available as we waited for our parents to finish working.

Although I loved my younger relatives dearly, I began to abhor the idea of childcare because it was always my assumed and unrecompensed responsibility. It should be noted that I am not completely heartless when it comes to little tykes; I regularly fawn over chubby cheeks and impossibly tiny onesies and remarkably sensible kid logic. What dismays me is the notion of sole responsibility, rancid odors, and the feasibility of sudden emergency. Be that as it may, often desperate times call for a change in heart.

While battling the college conflict, I was working full time at a sporting goods store and quickly worked my way up the corporate ladder. Then calamitous circumstances arose, and the company I worked for went bankrupt. Luckily, I was recruited right away by a competing sporting goods company and was hired at a higher position with an alluring raise.

This job, however, only lasted me a few months. With the closure of my former company and an additional well-known sporting goods company, my new employer became the prominent corporation and experienced a surplus of customer traffic. In poor judgment, the bigwigs attempted to further increase profit margins by severely cutting payroll.

Constant streams of irritable customers combined with an incommodious schedule culminated in superfluous amounts of stress among my team. We were also hit with an additional monumental wave of business when our local NBA and NHL teams both qualified for championship games within weeks of each other; to make matters worse, false advertisement broadcasted that we were the only retailer selling the limited-edition championship products. To keep up with our biweekly truck shipments, I would be scheduled to work at least one graveyard shift a week on top of my regular shifts. Quickly, I metamorphosed into a perpetually cranky hot mess.

I approached my management team—as well as the lower-level corporate managers—to authorize much-needed supplementary payroll. Instead I was met with the instruction to "work smarter *and* harder." I was outraged. My employees looked to me for alleviation from all the stress and tension that was out of my control. Meanwhile, I looked to my management team for assistance, but they were too busy trying to impress their corporate superiors. This stage of my life taught me that you cannot change what you refuse to confront, but when what you confront refuses to change, then it is time to let go and let God handle it.

Verse for Thought

"I hope, Lord. My whole being hopes, and I wait
for God's promise." (Psalm 130:5 CEB)

Reflection Question

What is something that you are uncertain about and need God's
clarity for?

Let Us Pray

Lord,
As I wait for Your will,
I look to You.
I need more of You, Father.
I know that I do not need to worry, for You hold
my future.
Until You reveal when and what that is,
I will trust in You and seek You out.
Amen.

8

Soul Windows

Resilience because of consequences from priorities

Our priorities are windows into our souls. They are reflections of what our hearts beat for. They can be found on the pages of our calendars and in the recently opened tabs of our computers. If our priorities are not placed on a solid foundation, they *will* lead us down a destructive, unfulfilling path.

Part of my responsibility as class president in high school was to lead the entire senior class in a devotional every month before our class meetings. I would typically begin my devotionals with a clever anecdote and then follow up with analogous Bible verses. When I came across the following story on the internet, I knew that I needed to share it with the class (with all the proper props!):

> A professor stood before his class and had some items in front of him. When the class began, wordlessly, he picked up a very large and empty mayonnaise jar and proceeded to fill it with golf balls. He then asked the students if the jar was full. They agreed that it was. The professor then picked up a box of pebbles and poured them into the jar. He shook the jar lightly. The pebbles rolled into the open areas between the golf balls. He then asked the students again if the jar was full. They agreed it was. The professor next picked up a box

of sand and poured it into the jar. Of course, the sand filled up everything else. He asked once more if the jar was full. The students responded with a unanimous "yes."

The professor then produced two cups of coffee from under the table and poured the entire contents into the jar, effectively filling the empty space between the sand. The students laughed.

"Now," said the professor, as the laughter subsided, "I want you to recognize that this jar represents your life. The golf balls are the important things—family, children, health, friends, and favorite passions—things that if everything else was lost and only they remained, your life would still be full. The pebbles are the other things that matter like your job, house, and car. The sand is everything else—the small stuff. If you put the sand into the jar first," he continued, 'there is no room for the pebbles or the golf balls.

"The same goes for life. If you spend all your time and energy on the small stuff, you will never have room for the things that are important to you. So … pay attention to the things that are critical to your happiness. Play with your children. Take time to get medical checkups. Take your partner out to dinner. There will always be time to clean the house and fix the disposal. Take care of the golf balls first—the things that really matter. Set your priorities. The rest is just sand."

One of the students raised her hand and inquired what the coffee represented. The professor smiled. "I'm glad you asked. It just goes to show you that no matter how full your life may

seem, there's always room for a couple of cups of
coffee with a friend."

The story was a smash; it ended in a laugh and left me with
a Mason jar full of mud. I replayed the visual representation and
permanently engraved the meaning in my mind as I scraped the
coffee-stained sand out of the jar grooves and into the sink. I
decided then and there that if God is gracious enough to bless me
with so much, I will strive to pleasingly prioritize them.

Although my job had provided me with substantial amounts
of money, the by-products from the workplace—stress, anxiety,
bitterness, impatience, perpetual fatigue—were not worth it. It
taught me that when the sole ambition in employment is to earn
money, then happiness becomes hard to come by. I had abandoned
my reliance on God and His commandment to "keep your lives
free from the love of money, and be content with what you have
because He has said, 'I will never leave you; I will always be by
your side'" (Hebrews 13:5 The Voice). Additionally, I had wasted
so much time making a living that I had neglected to make a life
for myself; I had overlooked the importance of budgeting time
for friends and family. Without people, how could I fulfill my
purpose?

For my next job venture, I desired employment in a positive
environment where the emphasis was on the people, not merely
on making money. That is when I remembered a lesser-known,
local chain of sporting goods stores that used to host my team's
track and field parties in high school. This particular company
sells brand-new sporting goods equipment at discounted prices
and donates 10 percent of their annual profits to a lengthy list of
local schools and charities.

Finally, I had found a corporate-less corporation that focused
on people and giving back instead of on policies and profits. One
of my friends from church worked there and had nothing but
good things to say about his job, so I applied. Ironically, they were

opening up a new location in the same city where I had opened (and closed) a store for my first job. Three relaxed interviews later, I accepted a base level, minimum-wage position at the new location. *I'm not here for the money,* I told myself. *I have new priorities now.*

Although I had finally achieved the emotional victory of abolishing "making buckets of money" from my list of priorities, I still needed to pay my bills. I swallowed my pride and applied to additionally work part time at the preschool of my family's school as an aide alongside my mom. My shocked, close friends and family asked, "But don't you hate kids …?"

Despite all my presaged skepticism, I was pleasantly surprised by my experience after only a short time. My predominant role was to act as a supervisor out in the hallway during potty breaks, but I also had the daily opportunity to pull kids aside individually and help their fine motor skills burgeon through fun activities. It was nice being recognized as a leader again and feeling depended on. With the added bonus of getting to work alongside my mom, I was beginning to consider the possibility of becoming a teacher.

In order to comply with licensing requirements for becoming an official preschool teacher, I needed to take four early childhood education classes. Taking four courses at my community college would mean full-time student status, but I was already working part time at the school on top of full time at the sporting goods store. I decided to temporarily pause working at the school to earn my credentials through night school after my shifts at the store.

Then curiosity led me to begin exploring the idea of taking the plunge and earning my full-on bachelor degree. I decided that an online program would best benefit me, because I would not have to worry about relocating or sacrificing more of my schedule. My research led me to a private university in Arizona that offered several programs that interested me. Intrigued, I filled out one of the *Want to Know More?* forms and anxiously waited to hear back.

I quickly received a greeting from a counselor who graciously answered all my questions and informed me of a visit day that they were hosting the following week. It was an all-expenses-paid trip to the school for the day where I could meet the deans and get a feel for the campus. The whole excursion sounded nice but unnecessary considering that I just wanted to participate in their online program. On the other hand, my best friend from high school attended the school, so I signed up for the trip thinking that at the very least it was a free adventure and I could visit my friend.

When the day arrived, my family drove me to the airport at three in the morning, and I checked in to the airline indicated on the itinerary that the school had emailed to me. Panic surged through me as I realized that it was beginning to storm intensely outside. After my boarding group was called, I nervously stepped into the swaying plane. One distinct and dismal thought rang in my head over and over again as I sat down and buckled up: *If this plane takes off, we are all going to die.* I sent a text to my brother saying that it was nice knowing him.

As the remaining passengers boarded and settled in, the flight attendants began to pace the wavering aircraft, whispering to one another, "The captain says that the first half hour is going to be rough, so be ready." Right on time, the pilot came over the intercom and briefed us on the takeoff procedures, but as he revved up the engines, the cabin quickly filled with the rancid odor of gasoline. The pilot immediately switched off the plane, and he instructed us to stay calm as the crew investigated the issue.

Five minutes later, the pilot came back on the intercom to address the nervous crowd. "Alright, we were not able to locate the origin of the odor, but we are going to try this one more time and see what happens." He talked us through the takeoff procedures once more, and as soon as he turned on the engines, the cabin once again filled with the unmistakable stench of gasoline.

The pilot calmly but firmly told us to quickly gather our things so that we could evacuate the aircraft. Panicked mothers and annoyed businessmen filed into the aisle and attempted to inch their way closer to the door, but to no avail. A few minutes passed, and the pilot once again came over the intercom to warn us that the grounds crew had broken the jet bridge as they hurried it back to the plane door. When the door was finally opened, we had to jump down about two feet to reach the bridge. Sideswept rain soaked everyone through to the skin.

We lined up one by one at the terminal service desk to get reassigned new flights. Upon my turn, I was informed that the next flight would take off three hours later. Concerned that I would miss too many of my scheduled meetings, I called the school's travel hotline. They told me that delays happened all the time and to hang tight until the next flight. Fortunately, I had become friends with a fellow passenger who happened to live on the same street as my new workplace, so I had someone to keep me company.

After waiting an hour, the school called me back and told me to forget it. By the time I would arrive on campus, there would only be an hour and a half before I needed to leave to return to the airport. I had my ticket cancelled and asked my family to pick me up. Due to the storm, it would be another two hours before they could even get to the airport, so they told me to take a train home. Ironically, the train broke down along the way.

Travel experiences like this one have become common occurrences for me. I have learned that each ordeal offers a unique lesson, but I was struggling to pinpoint the significance of this particular event. When I got home, I spent the remainder of the day pondering why I was even researching schools. I had not gone to any of my classes that week. When I was in class, I would just play games in my head to entertain myself; my notebooks contained tally marks of how many times my teachers would say "um" and polls of how many people I noticed that were left-handed versus right-handed.

My parents were the main reason that I kept attempting to

continue my college education. While I have lived the fun parts of life by pursuing the planted passions that bloom inside my heart, I have lived the serious parts by being a people pleaser. I pursued physical therapy because my dad wanted me to become a doctor, and later I pursued teaching because my mom wanted me to become a teacher.

Yet spending thousands of dollars on an education consisting of sitting in a classroom listening to lectures for hours and mindlessly recording verbatim on exams was not what *I* wanted for myself. I did not want to sit in a classroom anymore. I wanted to travel the world and meet new people and learn about cultures firsthand. School had administered me negative connotations for learning with the pressures of class rankings and structured curriculum. Meanwhile, my traveling adventures were teaching me about the importance of loving other people and honoring our differences.

I was finally happy.

Or so I thought.

Verse for Thought

> "Really, what profit is there for you to gain the whole world and lose yourself *in the process*?" (Mark 8:36 The Voice)

Reflection Question

What are your priorities?

Let Us Pray

> *God,*
> *Sometimes it feels like I have no time,*
> *But I dedicate myself to make time.*
> *Help me organize my schedule,*
> *So that I yield to Your ways,*
> *So that I prioritize people,*
> *So that my work honors You.*
> *You are worthy of it all.*
> *Amen.*

9

Why I Dropped Out of College
Resilience because of consequences from persistence

That was the original title of this book.

Why I Dropped Out of College.

I indignantly filled pages of a notebook with my haughty thoughts on how I knew best. But as I wrote, I noticed that I was still losing sleep. I was still feeling unfulfilled.

I read statistics about inspiring celebrities like Steve Jobs, Mark Zuckerberg, Walt Disney, Kanye West, and Oprah Winfrey, who all created successful lives without a college diploma.

I fought the culminating thoughts that screamed at me, "You are a quitter!" And I believed them. *I am a quitter,* I gave in. *In one year alone, I have held five jobs and accumulated eight W's on my transcript.* I neglected to remember John Sinclair's words—that "failure is a temporary bruise, not a permanent tattoo." No, not on God's precious creation.

I was striving to achieve what the magnificent writer Beau Taplin considers to be what is most important of all: to have found my passion in my workplace. "It is absolutely essential you find a way to obtain the same level of satisfaction from your work as you do from your free time. To live for the weekend is, after all, to waste away 71.43% of your life."

But after too many years of fighting this continual internal war, I now realize that the battle I was fighting was the wrong one and all for naught. I spent too long trying to ask myself, *What do* I *want to be when I grow up?* when I should have been asking, *God, what do* You *want me to be when I grow up?* As the great Oswald Chambers said, "As Christians, we are not here for our own purpose at all—we are here for the purpose of God, and the two are not the same."

We still need a vision, yes. The sage Solomon said that, "where there is no vision, the people perish ..." (Proverbs 19:18a JKV). But he finished the same sentence with, "but those who adhere to God's instruction know *genuine* happiness" (Proverbs 19:18b The Voice). As we make it through manic Mondays and hump day Wednesdays, we should never overlook the significance of our self-worth, our passions, our desires, our dreams, our visions. The key, dear friend, is to tether our pursuits to the purpose of God. When we align our hearts to that formula, He will shower our lives in the endless energy and the relentless resolve it takes to change the world.

Jesus was tempted by the enemy with the same struggle that plagued me and has beleaguered many others both now and over the course of thousands of years: to settle for less than God's best.

> Then the devil gave Jesus a vision. It was as if He traveled around the world in an instant and saw all the kingdoms of the world at once.
>
> Devil: All these kingdoms, all their glory, I'll give to You. They're mine to give because this whole world has been handed over to me. If You just worship me, then everything You see will all be Yours. All Yours!
>
> Jesus: [Get out of My face, Satan!] The Hebrew Scriptures say, "Worship and serve the Eternal One your God—only Him—and nobody else." (Luke 4:5–8 The Voice)

We are called to be *in* this world and not *of* it (see John 17:14). Our enemy's goal is to trap us in it, because this is his turf. He has the home court advantage ... for now. Sure, he can tempt us and show us a lifetime of riches, but they will not carry over into eternity. The climb up a corporate ladder does not carry over into eternity either.

Jesus resisted the enemy's temptations and instead insisted on the reality of God's truths. The Bible assures that we can do all things through Christ (see Philippians 4:13); it assures us that we are more than conquerors (see Romans 8:37). As A. W. Tozer said, "How completely satisfying it is to turn from our limitations to a God who has none."

Our focus does not need to be on exerting all our efforts on building our careers. God will open doors when and where He sees fit.

Jesus did not get caught up in pursuing a career in carpentry. Matthew did not hesitate to give up his seat as a tax collector. Simon Peter dropped his nets that were full of fish.

Why?

Because those occupations weren't their true callings. Jesus called them to follow Him wherever He led.

There is a time for everything. Or as The Byrds sang, "To everything (turn! turn! turn!) there is a season (turn! turn! turn!) and a time to every purpose under heaven."

Our momentum and pace in life are never constant and are often interrupted, yet "we are confident that God is able to orchestrate everything to work toward something good and beautiful when we love Him and accept His invitation to live according to His plan" (Romans 8:28 The Voice).

The challenge, often, is in the waiting. I like to plan everything out; I want an accurate minute-by-minute timeline for meals, an achievable, by-the-penny budget for my finances, and a perfectly mapped out mile-for-mile itinerary for each of my international journeys. I, like so many other people in this day and age of fast and free delivery and mobile app preordering, want things *now*. Yet, as you may have noticed, God does not work on a here-and-now kind of timeline. On day eight, He did not create an app that allows us to simply tap prayer emojis with instant results. God is not Santa.

As kids growing up in a Christian school, my classmates and I would always argue about the age-old chicken and the egg scenario. *Which came first, the chicken or the egg?* We would debate over and over again. Either way, aren't you glad that today it is always the egg that comes first?

Every creature, every human enters this world with a beautiful beginning full of hope and possibility. Then, when God appoints, we emerge into our roles. We transform from led to leaders and from taught to teachers, because as sheep we faithfully follow our Shepherd. The key is just to wait for His anointing appointments. He made all the greats wait:

Joseph waited thirteen years.

Abraham waited twenty-five years.

Moses waited forty years.

Jesus waited thirty years.

"Meanwhile, the moment we get tired in the waiting, God's Spirit is right alongside helping us along" (Romans 8:26 MSG). He never abandons us. In fact, while we are waiting, He is strengthening us; He is busy reinforcing the necessary components within us so that when the time comes, we will be unstoppable!

Joshua waited alongside Moses for those forty years. He did not come out of the womb swinging his sword. Instead, Joshua endured the typical training. He learned how to become a godly leader by faithfully leading the army of Israel through the wilderness with the Eternal as his battle flag (see Exodus 17:15). It was through these victories that God was preparing Joshua for his anointing appointment and defining defeat: the conquest of the promised land.

When the time came, Moses passed on his title and this

wisdom to Joshua: "Be strong and brave! You're going to lead these people into the land the Eternal promised their ancestors He'd give them. You'll give it to them, and they'll give it to their descendants. And He will be leading you. He'll be with you, and He'll never fail you or abandon you. So don't be afraid!" (Deuteronomy 31:7b–8 The Voice).

After Jesus had ascended back into heaven, He had the disciples do some waiting of their own. "He had instructed His chosen messengers through the Holy Spirit, prohibiting them from leaving Jerusalem, but rather requiring them to wait there until they received what He called 'the promise of the Father'" (Acts 1:3b–4 The Voice).

So they obeyed. They went to the upper room—their waiting room—and as they waited, they prayed. "This whole group devoted themselves to constant prayer with one accord" (Acts 1:14a The Voice).

How beautiful is that response? Jesus declared that His disciples wait, so they decided to devote themselves to prayer!

Friend, if you find yourself waiting in your own upper room, do not lose hope! Your season of waiting may feel like an eternity, but take courage. Listen to King David's instruction: "Don't give up. Wait for the Eternal in expectation, and be strong. Again, wait for the Eternal" (Psalm 27:14 The Voice).

Your waiting is conditioning your spirit while God is strengthening your heart. So seek Him out. Praise in earnest and pray with fervor. Jesus promised these encouraging words about effective prayer, "Keep on asking, and you will receive what you ask for. Keep on seeking, and you will find. Keep on knocking, and the door will be opened to you" (Matthew 7:7 NLT).

The upper room was not the first time that the disciples had found themselves behind closed doors.

On that same evening (Resurrection Sunday), the followers gathered together behind locked doors in fear that some of the Jewish leaders in Jerusalem were still searching for them. Out of nowhere, Jesus appeared in the center of the room.

Jesus: May each one of you be at peace.

As He was speaking, He revealed the wounds in His hands and side. The disciples began to celebrate as it sank in that they were really seeing the Lord.

Jesus: I give you the gift of peace. In the same way the Father sent Me, I am now sending you.

Now He drew close enough to each of them that *they could feel His breath*. He breathed on them:

Jesus: Welcome the Holy Spirit of the living God. You now have the mantle of God's forgiveness. As you go, you are able to share the life-giving power to forgive sins, or to withhold forgiveness. (John 20:19–23 The Voice)

Wow! Jesus appeared—*He showed up*—even when the doors were locked; even when the disciples thought that He was dead; even when they felt abandoned and were hiding. But still Jesus came and turned a situation of fear into a launching pad for forgiveness.

How often do we spend time behind locked doors cowering in fear instead of waiting in eager anticipation? I know that I do *way* too much. Just last week, my pastor felt led by the Holy Spirit during the Sunday service to speak a prophetic word over my future. He spoke such encouraging promises that I should have started running through the streets filled with joy. But instead I rushed straight to my house, locked the door, closed the drapes, and pulled the sheets over my head. The future felt so threatening because I have been so accustomed to figuring it out on my own.

But when the time comes, and God answers your knocking, do not keep the doors locked! Declare that you are no longer a slave to fear, a slave to figuring out your own future. Waltz into this new beginning with the blessing of Jesus: "May each one of you be at peace."

Verses for Thought

> "Why would you ever complain, O Jacob, or, whine, Israel, saying, 'God has lost track of me. He doesn't care what happens to me'? Don't you know anything? Haven't you been listening? God doesn't come and go. God *lasts*. He's Creator of all you can see or imagine. He doesn't get tired out, doesn't pause to catch his breath. And he knows *everything*, inside and out. He energizes those who get tired, gives fresh strength to dropouts. For even young people tire and drop out, young folk in their prime stumble and fall. But those who wait upon God get fresh strength. They spread their wings and soar like eagles, They run and don't get tired, they walk and don't lag behind." (Isaiah 40:30–31 MSG)

Reflection Questions

What is something God is having you wait on?

Is your upper room full of fear or eager anticipation?

Let Us Pray

> *Lord,*
> *As I wait, I trust in You.*
> *Give me vision, Lord—*
> *One that extends far beyond myself,*
> *A vision that will draw others to You,*
> *A vision that will last into eternity with You.*
> *Amen.*

10

Previously on *I Didn't Know I Was Pregnant* ...

Resilience because of consequences from obedience

This last month of my life was like being on that show *I Didn't Know I Was Pregnant*, then suddenly starting an orphanage, and then having to brokenheartedly give away all my babies. I was not the one pregnant, no. My two adopted cats were. One mama had five babies and the other mama had six. Suddenly, the girl who fervently hates cats had thirteen of them!

How did this all start, you ask? It began when my next-door neighbors adopted two kittens. Everyone in the neighborhood was thrilled ... except for me. Due to sudden circumstances, my neighbors moved to a different location that did not allow cats.

The orange and gray kittens began roaming into our yard in search of food daily. Enraged with my hatred for cats, I instructed my mother and brother to *never* feed the cats under any circumstances. I knew that once they were given food, they would pitch their tent stakes and never leave. Boy, was I right that they would never leave, and boy, was I wrong to think that it would be my mother and brother who would feed them!

My hatred for cats is rooted back to my early childhood years. After my parents' divorce, my mom let us adopt a cat. He was not intended to be a replacement for my dad, but merely a distraction or an addition to the family. Our tabby, Roger, was quickly smothered in love and affection, but to my dismay, he did not return any to me. He loved my mom; he would cuddle and purr with her all the time. When I tried to force him to love me, he would not have it (surprise, surprise). Instead, he would repay me in scratches and would eat my pet goldfishes.

For years, I pestered my mom to let me have my own cat, a cat that would only love *me*. "We already have a cat!" she would argue.

I would counter, "But he hates meeeeee!" My mom finally relented, and I happily went to the pet store to pick out my new friend. I ironically picked out a female, orange cat named Ginger. I locked her in my room and made sure that she saw me as her sole food provider. *Surely she will love only me*, I thought.

Since the cat was not as naive as I believed her to be (or as naive as I was), she still recognized my mom as the alpha of the family and didn't give a rat's behind about me. Additionally, my brother interrupted my plan by coming in periodically to give love and affection to the adorable little feline. Ginger apparently did not like him either and would scratch her way out of any situation that did not involve our mom. To our surprise, my brother's scratches would swell and turn tomato red every time. It turns out my brother is allergic to long-haired cats.

To add to all the fun, my room was intoxicatingly potent with the sour smell of urine all day, every day. I assumed that because she was an older cat that maybe she was just adjusting to her new home, but it never ended. She would not even stop playing to pee; she just started whizzing away as she relentlessly pawed at her toys. Something was wrong.

It turned out that she had a severe urinary tract infection that was incurable, and the pound insisted that we surrender her back to them. I was heartbroken. My brother's allergies were too severe for us to risk getting another cat, so I returned home eager to make Operation Make-Roger-Love-Me a success.

I eventually learned that kitty love cannot be forced, instead it is earned over time. He and I later enjoyed cuddle sessions and cat naps. Our bond was further strengthened when we sold our house and moved into the guest room of my grandparents' house. We three humans and one cat quite humorously made many memories together in that room until we finally found a new house. Roger was a trooper throughout the moving process and transitioned well alongside us.

In celebration of new beginnings, I wanted a new pet to match our new home. This time, I wanted a dog. I had longed for a dog for several years. To prove my seriousness and readiness for responsibility, I would drag my stuffed Lady from Disney's *Lady and the Tramp* around the block on a leash and then three times a day I would force-feed her small pebbles from our backyard. I brought her along on short car trips around town and would patiently wait in the car with her, peering out windows that were slightly cracked open "for proper ventilation for my dog."

The next summer, while my brother and I were away visiting our dad, my mom and aunt were busy perusing through newspapers and visiting pet shelters. My mom had given in and opened room in her heart for another pet. One day I received the text: they had found the perfect dog.

As soon as our plane landed at the end of the week, my brother and I excitedly scurried through security, dodged our way in and out of the baggage claim, and dragged our bags behind us through the parking lot. In the distance we could see a blonde, curly haired doggy happily sauntering toward us. My brother and I looked at each other with the same expression engraved on our faces: "He is so ugly … we love him!"

My mom had bought our new dog, Hunter, from a family in Pacheco who had found him wandering the streets. A vet visit informed us that he was at least three years old and was probably a cocker spaniel mixed with golden retriever. His curly hair and short but muscular stature agreed with that estimate.

Needless to say, Roger was not a fan of our new pet. Hunter

would curiously sniff, and Roger would territorially scratch. They had many duals in the backyard, and eventually Roger had it.

I will never forget the day that he decided to move on. Hunter had just playfully initiated another dual, and Roger walked away. As he did, he looked back at me, and his eyes bid me farewell. I knew. I ran after him to try to lock him away in my room and never let him go, but he hopped the fence into my neighbor's backyard.

Tears still stream down my face when I remember that look in his eye. He was so irritated with me, and I knew he would never come back. My mom was able to catch a glimpse of him every once in a while at my neighbor's house until we knew he was getting old and he was never seen again.

That's why I decided to hate cats. They sprung up too many painful memories, so I decided to dwell on the dog that I had and that was that. Until my neighbors moved away, abandoning their two new kittens.

I warned my family. "Don't feed them. They are evil!" I named them Sodom and Gomorrah, after the two ancient cities in the Bible that God smote off the face of the earth because they were so full of wickedness.

But one day, I received a text from my brother. It read, "The kittens are so hungry, I saw them eating the fence!" The small portion of my heart that wasn't hardened by brokenness ached. Coincidentally, my daily Bible scripture began with this short introduction:

> A person in a positive relationship with God stands in a right relationship with His creation. How we treat animals may mirror our souls— not just the pets in our home, but the pets in our neighborhood and the animals in our food supply. One who is truly right with God considers the needs of His creatures. (The Voice)

I gave in and sent a text out to everyone in my family: "Fine! I will feed the cats." I grabbed my keys and drove to Target. I set out determined to buy the cheapest bag of cat food that they had. To my surprise, a twisted sale made their biggest bag the cheapest, and I walked away with seventeen pounds of kitty kibble.

Our nosy neighborhood noticed right away that I had begun feeding them, and the rumor spread that I was claiming them. My haughty attitude from this weird chain of events was evident in my thought process: if I was going to be paying for their food, then I'm claiming them!

I fed them, and they grew. They would greet me in the driveway every day when I arrived home from work. I told my coworkers that I actually found it refreshing to come home to two beings who depended on me and were happy to see me (if only for the food that I would inevitably bring out). I felt like a real mom.

A few months later, I returned home from a trip to Guatemala. My first thought was *What the ... how did they get to be so fat?* I instantly instilled a mandatory diet. As a result, the cats would endlessly meow for more food and were terribly irritable.

I didn't understand what could be wrong until I came home one foggy evening to the sound of five faint little kazoos. Out of the corner of my eye, I noticed movement in my garden and shrieked because I thought we had an infestation of ugly, naked rat babies. My cats were equally as horrified, and their faces were terror-stricken.

Upon further inspection, I realized that those ugly, naked rat babies were actually freshly newborn kittens. It was near freezing outside, so I pounded on the door for my brother to wake up and help me bring them inside. As soon as we wrapped them in a blanket and placed them in a laundry basket on the dining room table, the kazoo shrieks ceased.

Our mom was at a church meeting and wasn't expected home for another couple of hours, so I remained frozen in place staring at the predicament that I was in. Eventually, I moved past shock and transitioned into a state of pure panic. Since Google has turned out to be my adulting survival guide, I spent hours trying to figure out exactly what my role as grandma to cats was going to look like.

All my research said the same thing: not to worry, the mom cat will do all the work. *Awesome! But which one is the mom ...* I wondered. I opened the front door to find both cats wide-eyed and worried. I picked up each cat and hovered them, one by one, over the kittens to see which one would demonstrate motherly behavior. The second cat purred instantaneously; Gomorrah was the mama.

Mama and her babies spent the first night in our bathroom. Further research taught me that the new family needed to live in a dark, undisturbed place. Our one, shared, tiny bathroom was probably not the right home for them, so I extended them an invitation to live in my bedroom. I went to Walmart and bought ample food, kitty litter, and a litter box.

Sodom gave birth a week later. I now had a grand total of thirteen cats, all living in my room. The first few weeks were easy. Both moms instinctively took great care of their babies. They groomed and fed their little ones all day; in turn I made sure both moms were fed, watered, and provided with fresh litter.

Everyone loved sneaking a peak at the tiny, blind babies. As they matured, we enjoyed watching as their small eyes cracked open and they explored the mysterious reality of color. Then their little legs strengthened, and they took their wobbly first steps. Soon walking turned into running ... with style. Step-step-step-step-*faceplant!* became the familiar awkward pattern of movement.

Hunter loved the kittens. He would patiently sit and peer into the laundry baskets as they slept. Once my mom, brother, and I all came home from work, then recess would commence! We would take out all the babies. Sodom and Gomorrah peacefully relaxed in the corner, and Hunter stressfully circled the kittens. He would nudge their behinds to encourage them to practice walking but then would have a puppy panic attack if they wandered outside of his circular perimeter.

The real fun started once their nails came in and their bowels matured. They learned to climb onto my bed and tore up the carpet and. They. Pooped. Everywhere. At this stage, I began to market them on social media and asked all my family and friends if anyone was interested in a free kitten.

My neighbor was the only taker. She agreed to take two kittens, but not until they were seven weeks old, the appropriate age to separate the babies from their mothers. One week before her deadline, I had enough. I had begun sleeping on the couch in the living room because the smell in my room became intolerable. My days were spent refilling water bowls, food bowls, and cleaning up endless amounts of poop. I had nothing but empathy for all mothers everywhere.

I was so close to corralling all thirteen cats into my Mini Cooper and dropping them off at the local animal shelter. Instead, I picked up my Bible and reread that passage about caring for animals. I renewed my dedication, and God strengthened my hands. He reminded me of my last trip to Guatemala where I had flirted with the idea of one day opening my own orphanage. I realized that these cats were the means that He was providing me with to perform a dress rehearsal. Instead of complaining that this was what happened when I tried to be a good person, I considered this to be a possible glimpse into my future. With "Jess's Orphanage" written in big letters across my door, I persevered another week.

Taking the cats to the pound was the hardest thing I had done. I fought tears as I filled out the necessary paperwork, but the waterworks unleashed once I reminisced about the time spent caring and playing with each cat. It was like giving away my own children. I cried so much that an officer came over to interview me to ensure that I was not being abused.

I have always been told that there are certain things that I will not fully understand until I have kids of my own. Things such as unconditional love, separation anxiety, and sacrifice. I think of the story in the Bible where God commanded Abraham to sacrifice his son Isaac.

Isaac was his long-awaited, promised son. God told Abraham to wait, and Abraham waited ... at first. Then he got antsy and took things into his own hands. But the Lord captured his attention, and Abraham renewed his dedication. His long-endured waiting was rewarded with the arrival of God's precious promise.

Then, just when you thought that we had reached our happy ending ... plot twist! God said, "Kill him!" Loving-Heavenly-Father-say-what? God instructed Abraham to offer Isaac as a burnt offering. "But God!" I counter. "He waited so long! This is his beloved son we are taking about!" Abraham did not use my selfish argument. Instead, he immediately obeyed, took Isaac up onto a mountain, and began the preparation.

Then, like the Bible version of *Gotcha!*, God interrupted the ceremony and provided an alternate sacrifice. A special messenger complimented Abraham: "I know now that you respect *the one True* God *and will be loyal to Him and follow His commands,* because you were willing to give up your son, your only son, to Me" (Genesis 22:12 The Voice). We see this same sacrificial love later when God Himself sacrificed His precious Son, Jesus, to die for you and me on the cross.

Now, I know that I only had kittens. But perspective, no matter how small, can open new levels of understanding and teach a powerful lesson by enacting empathy. We often consider God's timing to take longer than we would like, but "the Lord is not slow about enacting His promise—slow is how some people want to characterize it—*no, He is not slow* but patient *and merciful* to you, not wanting anyone to be destroyed, but wanting everyone to turn away from following his own path and to turn toward God's" (2 Peter 3:9 The Voice). Meanwhile, He sends us the means to renew our dedication as He strengthens our hands.

Verse for Thought

> "So then, my dear friends, stand firm and steady. Keep busy always in your work for the Lord, since you know that nothing you do in the Lord's service is ever useless." (1 Corinthians 15:58 GNT)

Reflection Question

What is it in your life that God is using to teach you in your season of waiting?

Let Us Pray

> *Lord,*
> *I know this circumstance is from You.*
> *I know that You are with me.*
> *Give me strength.*
> *Teach me more about Yourself through this.*
> *Amen.*

11

Put on Your Mickey Ears
Resilience because of consequences from boldness

I call my entire, extended family the Crazy Bunch. We do loud. We do fun. We do awesome. I started telling people that nothing embarrasses me anymore. Before you start listing off to me potentially embarrassing anecdotes to make me retract that statement, let me explain. I come from an entertainingly crazy family where at least one of the following circumstances will occur per family gathering:

We take a family selfie in a bathtub/shower (happens *way* more often than you would expect.).

We get kicked out by security.

We play croquet with plastic flamingos.

We get kicked out by security.

We dress up as Waldo from *Where's Waldo*'s evil twin, Odlaw, and stand in the middle of the Golden Gate Bridge.

We get kicked out by security (I'm assuming you sense the pattern, so I'll stop now).

We consider dangerous, collapsed caves to be playgrounds.

We take extensive trips to Disneyland where our party of fifteen strategically runs from ride to ride, totaling up to nine to twelve miles a day.

We draw names at Christmas and only give gag gifts that are tailored to make fun of the person that we drew.

We buy mannequins in San Francisco, carry them around

the city piece by piece, and take them home via trolley and the BART train.

We regularly ride elevators and escalators up and down until (surprise, surprise!) security kicks us out.

That is my family. We have reached pro status in passive aggression, won the gold medal in sarcasm, and would receive the million-dollar prize from *America's Funniest Home Videos* if only we had a film crew stalking us. Our exciting family adventures are always entertaining.

We are quite Disney-obsessed. Magical. Fairy-tale. Relaxing. Vacation. Happily ever after. These are most likely the words that come to mind when you think of your ideal visit to the happiest place on earth. But when the Crazy Bunch storms the castle, it's a whole new world! To say that my family simply loves Disney would be an understatement. For example, our last Christmas was Disney-themed with a few simple rules:

1. Only Disney presents
2. Only Disney decor
3. Only Disney games to play after opening presents
4. Only foods that would be found at a Disney park
5. Everyone had to wear something Disney

As you can imagine, Disney was everywhere.

I even worked at Walt Disney World in Orlando, Florida, for a short while. While I was training, my supervisors told me that every day the parks profit enough revenue from ice-cream sales to cover the payroll for every cast member. From *ice-cream sales*! It blows my mind how much money Disney makes. Net gain constantly pours in from all over the world due to television, cinema, music, cruise lines, theme parks, merchandise, and more.

During my time teaching preschool, it was nearly impossible to find a child without a Disney backpack or pair of light-up, Disney tennis shoes. Even at the orphanage that I worked at in

Guatemala, all the girls would twirl in their *Frozen* t-shirts singing "Let it Go." Right now, I am wearing a shirt from a Disney Tinker Bell half marathon.

Specifically in the theme parks, Mickey ears are very popular. Grandparents licking ice-cream cones, babies in strollers, mom and dad in line behind you, and all of the "cool kids" taking selfies in front of the castle are wearing 'em.

But you never see them worn anywhere else. If your neighbor wore them while she walked laps with her dog around the neighborhood, everyone would think it strange. If the guy in front of you at the checkout at the grocery store was wearing them, be honest, you would judge him so hard.

Sometimes wearing Mickey ears in public is what it feels like to be a Christian. It is easy at church where everyone else is wearing, saying, and doing the same things. But outside, where we feel alone, it seems harder. So we stash our Mickey ears in the back of our closets until next Sunday. We sit back. We let witnessing opportunities slide for the sake of "fitting in."

But we are not alone. Paul commands us to "draw [our] strength and might from God. Put on the full armor of God to protect yourselves from the devil and his evil schemes. We're not waging war against enemies of flesh and blood alone. No, this fight is against tyrants, against authorities, against *supernatural* powers *and demon princes that slither* in the darkness of this world, and against wicked *spiritual armies* that lurk about in heavenly places" (Ephesians 6:10b–12 The Voice).

This sounds an awful lot like the plot to an epic Disney princess movie! In fact, it sounds like basically every television and cinematic theme ever written. Actor and producer Kirk Cameron explains just that in his introduction to the text of his film *Kill the Dragon, Get the Girl.*

A Note to the Reader:

The story you are about to read is the story of the Bible. The story of killing the dragon and getting the girl. Think about it. In the Bible, who is the dragon? Who is the girl?*

In the world we live in, that story gets repeated over and over. Right now there are dragons to fight, and there are girls to save. This story will inspire you to take up that good fight and embark on that bold journey. Plus, it's just a whole lot of fun. It had me cracking up.

My family loves stories like this. We read them out loud around the dinner table, on the couch on a lazy Saturday, and in our pajamas, cozied in our beds. Stories like Kill the Dragon, Get the Girl are exactly the kind of stories I want shaping my kids. Their imaginations, their loyalties, their passions. I want the truths of the Bible getting deep into their bones, and stories that reenact those truths help.

—Kirk Cameron

*PS In the Bible, the dragon is Satan, that old serpent the Devil, who comes to steal, kill, and destroy. The girl is the bride of Christ, the Church, whom Jesus comes to save. Jesus is the original dragon slayer, who crushes the head of the serpent, rescues his bride, and one day will take her to live with him in paradise for all of eternity, having defeated darkness forever. Now you know where Hollywood movie scripts get their ideas from.

Jesus's story of courageous battling and victorious defeat is far better than "the good life." It is easy to crave a relaxing life, free from conflict and on a secluded island, but what good is a story without a hero and some butt whoopin'? The cool thing is that we are a part of the story. We are the girl! So we need to buckle up and get ready to be saved.

"And this is why you need *to be head-to-toe in* the full armor of God: so you can resist during these evil days and be fully prepared to hold your ground. Yes, stand—truth banded around your waist, righteousness as your chest plate, and feet protected in preparation to proclaim the good news of peace. Don't forget to raise the shield of faith above all else, so you will be able to extinguish flaming spears hurled at you from the wicked one. Take also the helmet of salvation and the sword of the Spirit, which is the word of God" (Ephesians 6:13–17 The Voice).

Since we are well-equipped, we need not hide our Mickey ears. We need not hide *with* our Mickey ears. God wants to use us. He wants to go crazy through us. But He can't if we keep retreating to Netflix. And Instagram. And YouTube. And Facebook.

Instead of merely consuming others' content, God wants to use us to create content for Him. "Be generous with the different things God gave you, passing them around so all get in on it: if words, let it be God's words; if help, let it be God's hearty help. That way, God's bright presence will be evident in everything through Jesus, and *he'll* get all the credit as the One mighty in everything—encores to the end of time. Oh, yes!" (1 Peter 4:10–11 MSG).

Verse for Thought

> "Just as each one has received a gift, use it to serve others, as good stewards of the varied grace of God." (1 Peter 4:10 CSB)

Reflection Questions

Think of a time when you were in a difficult situation and needed to put on your Mickey ears. Did you?

If you didn't, is it okay? What can you do to be better equipped for next time? (Hint: think "Armor of God.")

What is your gift?

What is one practical way that you can apply your gift this week?

Let Us Pray

> *Heavenly Father,*
> *Sometimes this world can be so scary.*
> *Sometimes this life can be so hard.*
> *But thank You for being a faithful God who constantly pursues us—*
> *who kills the dragon and gets the girl.*
> *Help me to be generous with the gifts that You have generously given me in this time that I have left.*
> *Amen.*

12

Christian Bubble

Resilience because of consequences from addictions

I was raised to believe that any song that wasn't played on K-LOVE, our local Christian radio station, was of the devil. Any movie rated above G was unacceptable. Video games rotted your brain. Drugs were bad. Dancing made you pregnant.

I did not know why; yet, I never questioned any of it. Until I turned eighteen, I was under the authority of my mom. What she said went, and that was that.

My mom was young, and she just wanted to protect us. So she kept us in the "Christian bubble." Our CD player only played Christian records. Classic Disney movies were replayed until we had every word memorized. We went to Christian schools. Church was our main weekend activity.

When I finally entered adulthood, I experienced the expected culture shock. I was introduced to "real" music and movies. I heard certain words for the first time, quickly learning that my family's version of swear words were not even swear words at all!

These revelations also came with the realization that I was very different from "everyone else." The combination of my faith and my sheltered upbringing alienated me as I simultaneously started school at a secular community college and began my first job out in "the real world."

To add to the fun, there is the case of my voice. For those of you who I have not yet had the pleasure of meeting, allow me to share with you my most prominent—and often most defining—attributes: I look like I am fifteen and sound like I am five. (Imagine if Minnie Mouse sucked helium. That is approximately my octave level.)

Being in my twenties, the combination of my youthful appearance and my soft voice are both a blessing and a curse. I have the ability to score the child discount at museums and movie theaters, but I often get referred to as "cutie," "sweetheart," and other attempted endearing but derogatory nicknames.

When you throw my Christian upbringing into the mix, then I get identified as "the innocent one" who everyone works hard at protecting and preserving. "Earmuffs, Jess!" is the warning I receive before my coworkers spew profanity. I do not get invited to hangouts or parties. Conversations often hush when I walk up and the mood will change, spurring a shift in my insecurity.

I honestly do appreciate the respect for my faith and the apparent sense of responsibility that friends and strangers take upon themselves to preserve my naiveté, but it can sometimes be frustrating as I navigate the newness of the real world. Especially now that I have a new nine-year-old stepbrother. He's into Harry Potter and SpongeBob SquarePants. Both are things that I was never allowed to watch.

I recently bought a new carbon-fiber road bike from my workplace. After riding it for a few days, I brought it into the shop for an initial tune-up. While examining my bike, the mechanic asked me why I didn't bring it in sooner. Apparently, the brakes were not connected properly. "You should have felt that!" the mechanic told me, his eyebrow raised.

But I had no idea. I had never owned a fancy bicycle before. I felt like an idiot, just like I did when I tried supportive running shoes for the first time and was asked to describe the difference between my old Chucks and the new stability shoes. It left me speechless.

It seemed as though I would never be able to make my way

around in this new real world. How could I be a positive influence on others as a Christian if I could not even hold a normal conversation with them about Harry Potter or running shoes? The Bible says to "always be ready to offer a defense, humbly and respectfully, when someone asks why you live in hope" (1 Peter 3:15 The Voice). How can I do that when I have no idea what anyone is ever talking about?

But then peace washes over me when I remember these precious words from Jesus: "Make up your mind right now not to worry about it. I'll give you the words and wisdom that will reduce all your accusers to stammers and stutters" (Luke 21:14b–15 MSG).

Now, that does not mean that the Holy Spirit is going to suddenly sprinkle my conversations with references to Dumbledore and Voldemort. It doesn't. I know that because I had to use Google just now to even come up with those names! What we can expect, though, is the ability to live in this world without fear of falling into its misleading ways because Jesus is with us.

We cannot change the world by being like it. Jesus didn't! Instead, He was a countercultural radical who poured out an all-inclusive, nonexclusive love. He hung out with sinners—promiscuous prostitutes, thieving tax collectors, and indisposed drunks—on a regular basis.

> Later Jesus and his disciples were at home having supper with a collection of disreputable guests. Unlikely as it seems, more than a few of them had become followers. The religion scholars and Pharisees saw him keeping this kind of company and lit into his disciples: "What kind of example is this, acting cozy with the riffraff?"
>
> Jesus, overhearing, shot back, "Who needs a doctor: the healthy or the sick? I'm here inviting the sin-sick, not the spiritually-fit." (Mark 2:16–18 MSG)

Jesus went to parties with sinners, but He did not sin with the partygoers. Instead, He welcomed them, loved them, and transformed them. He was interested in change and offered them a chance to receive new identities and live new lives.

How can we do the same?

How can we wisely maneuver through our means of *media*, *music*, and *money* to bring a change to our generation?

The Bible talks a lot about putting off the old man/the dead man/the old life and embracing the new. "You've gotten rid of the person you used to be and the life you used to live, and you've become a new person. This new person is continually renewed in knowledge to be like its Creator" (Colossians 3:9b–10 NOG).

The content that we consume matters. Everything that we see, hear, and read on the news, on Tumblr, on Pinterest, on Netflix, on Hulu, on Facebook, on billboards, in magazines, via emails— *everything matters*. And we have control over it. To subscribe is to consent. You consent to receive those images. You consent to receive the propaganda. You consent to the words that leap from the pages and from the screens and into your mind.

Do not get me wrong here, friend. Don't think that you need to go crazy and delete all your social media accounts and unsubscribe from all your followings! Because I check Instagram and binge-watch Netflix just as much as the next person. (Actually, probably more. Like, *way* more …) Social media itself is not the problem. The Bible says to "think about the things that are good and worthy of praise. Think about the things that are true and honorable and right and pure and beautiful and respected" (Philippians 4:8 NCV). There are so many great streams of positive and encouraging content out there that will allow you to float deeper into the vast, wide ocean of God's promises.

The key is to decipher between what is good and what is destructive. The sinful issues that have woven themselves through our modern social media stem back to the ancient lie in the Garden of Eden amid the hearts of Adam and Eve: that God was holding them back, *that better is out there.* If we just take one bite, then think about all the knowledge that would be opened up to us!

From there, it spiraled out of control for generation after generation. It had become such a problem that years later, God had to set up some ground rules for the Israelites atop Mount Sinai. One of which was not to covet. "No lusting after your neighbor's house—or wife or servant or maid or ox or donkey. Don't set your heart on anything that is your neighbor's" (Exodus 20:17 MSG).

Our devices have screens that act as black mirrors. They make it hard for us to see exactly who we are and what we already have. Instead, it blurs and filters and shows us what we don't have, *that better is out there.* The grass seems so much greener on the other side.

So we log on for the twenty-second time today.

Because adding more friends? *That's better than what we already have.*

Because obtaining more knowledge? *That's better than what we already have.*

Because gaining more acceptance? *That's better than what we already have.*

We can defend social media platforms and streaming sites by calling them mere modes of entertainment, but the *Merriam-Webster* dictionary defines entertainment as an "amusement or diversion provided especially by performers." Media is a diversion from seeing what we already have.

We have a God who intentionally plants people into our lives (see Genesis 2:18).

We have a God who shares His knowledge with us (see Proverbs 2:6).

We have a God who accepts us, just as we are, even in our sinful state (see 1 Timothy 1:15).

What could be better than that? He always provides. Even Jesus's first miracle was one of provision:

Three days later, they all went to celebrate a wedding feast in Cana of Galilee. Mary, the mother of Jesus, was invited together with Him and His disciples. While they were celebrating, the wine ran out; and Jesus' mother hurried over to her son.

Mary: *The host stands on the brink of embarrassment; there are many guests, and* there is no more wine.

Jesus: Dear woman, is it our problem *they miscalculated when buying wine and inviting guests?* My time has not arrived.

But she turned to the servants.

Mary: Do whatever my son tells you.

In that area were six *massive* stone water pots that could each hold 20 to 30 gallons. They were typically used for Jewish purification rites. Jesus's instructions *were clear*:

Jesus: Fill each water pot with water until it's ready to spill over the top; then fill a cup, and deliver it to the headwaiter.

They did exactly as they were instructed. After tasting the water that had become wine, the headwaiter couldn't figure out where such wine came from (even though the servants knew), and he called over the bridegroom *in amazement.*

Headwaiter: *This wine is delectable.* Why would you save the most exquisite fruit of the vine? A host would generally serve the good wine first and, when his inebriated guests don't notice or care, he would serve the inferior wine. You have held back the best for last.

Jesus performed this miracle, the first of His signs, in Cana of Galilee. *They did not know how this happened,* but when the disciples *and the servants* witnessed this miracle, their faith blossomed. (John 2:1–11 The Voice)

Jesus provided a better wine than what had originally run out. It was not His intention for his friends and family to simply enjoy the cheap wine. Once inebriated, inferior wine is an easy addiction. Likewise, it is not Jesus's intention for us, His dearly loved children, to simply enjoy the distractions of this world. Once inebriated, too many TV show episodes and bottomless internet feed become an easy addiction.

> Therefore, as a witness of the Lord, I insist on this: that you no longer walk in the outsiders' ways— with minds devoted to worthless pursuits. They are blind to *true* understanding. They are strangers and aliens to the kind of life God has for them because they live in ignorance *and immorality* and because their hearts are *cold,* hard stones. And now, since they've lost all *natural* feelings, they have given themselves over to sensual, greedy, and reckless living. They stop at nothing to satisfy their impure appetites …

Just like any physical addiction, an approval addiction will demand your dependence upon it. You will suffer from extreme, emotional side effects. You will start to feel numb, unimportant, inferior.

> But this is not the path of the Anointed One, which you have learned. If you have heard Jesus and have been taught by Him according to the truth that is in Him, then you know to take off your former way of life, your *crumpled* old self—*that dark blot*

of a soul corrupted by deceitful desire and lust—
to take a fresh breath and to let God renew your
attitude and spirit. Then *you are ready to* put on
your new self, modeled after the very likeness of
God: truthful, righteous, and holy. (Ephesians
4:17–24 The Voice)

Obey Jesus's command and cleanse the old temptations and
distractions out of your life. Allow Jesus to provide a fulfilling,
ever-quenching peace. Enforce a change and experience the relief.
The next time you find yourself mind-numbingly trolling on
Facebook or taking stock of likes on past Instagram posts, direct
your search for affirmation from digital approval to the open arms
of the Maker of heaven and earth. When you give up addictions—
limit yourself to watching *one* season a day (uh, I mean week ...),
take a social media Sabbath, unsubscribe from junk email—you
may find that you have had better all along.

So here's what I want you to do, God helping you:
Take your every day, ordinary life—your sleeping,
eating, going-to-work, and walking-around life—
and place it before God as an offering. Embracing
what God does for you is the best thing you can
do for him. Don't become so well-adjusted to your
culture that you fit into it without even thinking.
Instead, fix your attention on God. You'll be
changed from the inside out. Readily recognize
what he wants from you, and quickly respond to
it. Unlike the culture around you, always dragging
you down to its level of immaturity, God brings
the best out of you, develops well-formed maturity
in you. (Romans 12:1–2 MSG)

Let us lift our eyes from the screens and use our hands to do more than scroll. Let us investigate our neighbors' needs. Talk to friends and exchange boisterous laughter instead of laugh-cry emojis. "Do your best to live a quiet life. Learn to do your own work well. We told you about this before. By doing this, you will be respected by those who are not Christians. Then you will not be in need and others will not have to help you" (1 Thessalonians 4:11–12 NLV). You will no longer live addicted to likes, because you belong to the One who loves you.

Verses for Thought

> "Looking at it one way, you could say, 'Anything goes. Because of God's immense generosity and grace, we don't have to dissect and scrutinize every action to see if it will pass muster.' But the point is not to just get by. We want to live well, but our foremost efforts should be to help *others* live well." (1 Corinthians 10:23–24 MSG)

Reflection Question

Who in your life—maybe a neighbor, coworker, coffee shop barista, hairdresser—can you help this week?

Let Us Pray

Lord God,
I have lost sight again, and I am sorry.
Amid the distractions in this world,
I choose You because You are better.
You did not redeem me so that I could merely live in a Christian bubble.
Make new wine out of me so that others can see Your goodness in me, Lord.
Amen.

13

Songs, Psalms, and Cinema
Resilience because of consequences
from consuming content

In high school, I was very into music (only Christian music, obviously, as that was the only genre that I knew even existed.). My friends and I delved into multiple different genres within the Christian music realm, and we attended probably around two hundred concerts. My favorite artists, though, hands down were the Christian rappers: Lecrae, Tedashi, Trip Lee, KB, anyone associated with the Christian 116 cliché.

After turning eighteen and becoming "my own, free person," I started listening to secular music. At first, I did not know where to start. Names like Michael Jackson, The Beatles, David Bowie, Drake, and Justin Timberlake were all foreign to me.

But as I dabbled, I was immediately drawn to secular hip-hop and R & B. It was what my new friends at work were listening to, and it sounded cooler than my old Christian rap music. Soon, it became my trademark. People loved it when I told them that my favorite music artist was Fetty Wap. With my high voice, no one expected it.

As I listened to my rap, I began experiencing new feelings. Rappers like Tupac, Eminem, and Jay-Z spoke lyrics about fatherlessness and abandonment that I could relate to. But dwelling in that sadness quickly led to a sticky bitterness that chained me down and consumed me. Although a lot of the music that I was listening to was in good fun and helped me relate to my colleagues, most of the lyrics silently held me captive.

It took several months of cutting away at the sticky strands of anger to finally break free from my addiction to bitterness. It can be so hard to let go sometimes, especially when it comes to emotions. But suppressing anger is like holding a beach ball captive underwater—inevitably it is going to explode. Luckily, the Bible provides a guideline and a timeline to combat against this sticky emotion: "When you are angry, don't let it carry you into sin. Don't let the sun set with anger in your heart or give the devil room to work" (Ephesians 4:26–27 The Voice).

Listen to the key words here: it is okay to be angry. Even Jesus expressed anger in a little temple tantrum! As He walked up the Southern Steps of the holy temple of Jerusalem preparing to worship, He was enraged when He saw merchants everywhere, barking out barters and exchange rates. But He did not allow His emotions to lead Him toward sin. Instead, He used His anger to defend God (see John 2:14–16 and Matthew 21:12).

Earlier on in the Bible, we see another example of anger—in fact, the very first appearance of anger—but this encounter was handled extremely differently. Adam and Eve, the OG humans, were living out their new, postgarden lives as farmers with their two sons, Cain and Abel. Cain gathered up some of his crops and offered them to God. Take note that this is before God established the laws requiring sacrifices, so kudos to Cain for his admirable act. Now Abel, he selects the best of the best from his elite, firstborn lambs and offers those up to God. Needless to say, God preferred the latter gift.

After all of this had transpired, "Cain became extremely angry and his face fell" (Genesis 4:5b The Voice). God noticed Cain's reaction.

Eternal One (to Cain): Why are you angry? And why do you look so despondent? *Don't you know that* as long as you do what is right, then I accept you? But if you do not do what is right, *watch out, because* sin is crouching at the door, ready to pounce on you! You must master it *before it masters you.* (Genesis 4:6–7 The Voice)

In the end, Cain let his anger get the best of him. He reacted in sin, in murder. Cain surrendered his heart to fury instead of forgiveness.

Forgiveness is the underlining theme here.

We were made not for forgetting wrongdoings, but *for giving* grace.

With God's help, I finally learned how to turn my bitterness from *fatherlessness* into *forgiveness.* And do you know what? Ultimately, the forgiveness toward my earthly father strengthened my *faithfulness* toward my heavenly Father.

Because God doesn't want there to be a divide.

God cares about families.

God cares about relationships.

God cares about generations.

He even hired John the Baptist to fill the position of a forerunner, a helper, a restorer—to prepare people's hearts for Jesus (see Luke 1:17). His ever-important job was prophesied over four hundred years beforehand, that he would "return parents' hearts to their children and children's hearts to their parents" (Malachi 4:6a The Voice). In Jesus's powerful parable of the prodigal son, we see this very principle. "The father looked off in the distance and saw the young man returning. He felt compassion for his son and ran out to him, enfolded him in an embrace, and kissed him" (Luke 15:20 The Voice).

Jesus reveals this simple truth:

God is the good, good Father.

His arms are open wide.

He desires to hold His children and whisper, "Welcome home."

This is the vital truth that so many people need to hear! It does not take long to hear the cry from fatherlessness on the hip-hop/R & B radio stations. Problematic paternal themes are common occurrences in cinema, too. Just look at some of the highest grossing films of 2017.

In *Star Wars: The Last Jedi*, Rey seeks answers about her parentage. Upon finding out that her thieving parents had abandoned her and died, Kylo Ren points out that Rey keeps attempting to patch her issues from fatherlessness by building relationships with Han Solo and Luke Skywalker. Peter Quill, also known as Star Lord, finally meets his absent father, Ego, in *Guardians of the Galaxy Vol. 2* and engages in a heartfelt game of catch with his dad. Later, however, when Ego's past and intentions are revealed, and Peter is forced to kill his father, Peter explains to his fellow guardian Rocket, "Well, of course I have issues. That's my freakin' father!" *Pirates of the Caribbean: Dead Men Tell No Tales*, the fifth film of the popular Disney pirate franchise, tells the story of two young children who thrust themselves into an epic adventure in search of their absent fathers. Do you see the pattern here?

I grew up watching *The Lion King*. I grew up crying with my companions while watching the tragic wildebeest scene. I grew up relating to Simba in losing a father. But later, I realized that I did not relate to Simba because of my earthly father, but my heavenly one.

Have you ever noticed how seemingly everyone in the Bible is compared to a lion? Jesus is the Lion of Judah (see Revelation 5:5). Our "enemy the devil is prowling around outside like a roaring lion, just waiting *and hoping for the chance* to devour someone" (1 Peter 5:8b The Voice). Wicked people of the world are "like young lions in their hiding places, they are poised to strike" (Psalm 17:9–12 The Voice). And we, Christians, are supposed to be the right-living, who "stand *their ground* as boldly as lions" (Proverbs 28:1 The Voice).

The kingdom that we live in sounds a lot like *The Lion King*, a lot like a lion kingdom. Especially because between both the kingdom of God and the lion kingdom, we have two heroic deaths and two heroic victories. In *The Lion King*, King Mufasa died to save his beloved son, Simba, from the clutches of the evil Scar; and *in the end, love prevails*. The kingdom of God exists because God's Son, Jesus, died to save His beloved sons and daughters (newsflash: that's you and me!) from the clutches of the evil Satan, and *in the end, love prevails*.

Death is not final. Movies like Disney Pixar's *Coco* and 20th Century Fox's *The Book of Life* share that same premise through their own unique tellings of Mexican tradition behind the Dia de los Muertos. During their adventures through the Land of the Dead, *Coco*'s family learns that life is less about seizing your moment than it is about family. In *The Book of Life*, Manolo is a young torero whose heart belongs to music, not bullfighting. During a fight, he sings "The Apology Song" to the bull, asking for forgiveness because "if you can forgive, *love can truly live*."

And we are back to the premise of the gospel: Jesus died to forgive our sins, proving that *love can truly live*. Death is something that we must do, too. Not just at the end of our lives, when our hearts stop, and we take our final breath. It is something we must do daily. Jesus left this challenge for His followers: "If anyone would come after me, let him deny himself and take up his cross daily and follow me" (Luke 9:23 ESV).

Why would Jesus ask us to do that? Why would He want us to die if He died to *save* us? It is because dead people don't worry about cash, careers, and clothes. Dead people don't obsess over looks and likes. Dead people don't constantly update, poke, tweet, post, and play next episode. My uncle has a license plate cover hanging in his garage that says, "He who dies with the most toys wins." But do you know what? Dead people can't play with those toys; they let go of everything.

Jesus knew that. That is why He wants us to die. "If you try to avoid danger and risk, then you'll lose everything. If you let go of your life and risk all for My sake, then your life will be rescued, *healed, made whole and full*. Listen, what good does it do you if you gain everything—if the whole world is in your pocket—but then your own life slips through your fingers and is lost to you?" (Luke 9:24–25 The Voice).

I love the way that Eugene H. Peterson rephrased Jesus's words:

> If you decide for God, living a life of God-worship, it follows that you don't fuss about what's on the table at mealtimes or whether the clothes in your closet are in fashion. There is far more to your life than the food you put in your stomach, more to your outer appearance than the clothes you hang on your body. Look at the birds, free and unfettered, not tied down to a job description, careless in the care of God. And you count far more to him than birds.
>
> Has anyone by fussing in front of the mirror ever gotten taller by so much as an inch? All this time and money wasted on fashion—do you think it makes that much difference? Instead of looking at the fashions, walk out into the fields and look at the wildflowers. They never primp or shop, but have you ever seen color and design quite like it? The ten best-dressed men and women in the country look shabby alongside them. If God gives such attention to the appearance of wildflowers— most of which are never even seen—don't you think he'll attend to you, take pride in you, do his best for you? What I'm trying to do here is to get you to relax, to not be so preoccupied with *getting,* so you can respond to God's *giving.* People who don't know God and the way he works fuss

over these things, but you know both God and how he works. Steep your life in God-reality, God-initiative, God-provisions. Don't worry about missing out. You'll find all your every day human concerns will be met.

Give your entire attention to what God is doing right now, and don't get worked up about what may or may not happen tomorrow. God will help you deal with whatever hard things come up when the time comes. (Matthew 6:25–34 MSG)

"For what is life?" the apostle Paul asked. "To me, it is Christ. Death, then, will bring more." (Philippians 1:21 GNT) More light, more love, more life. Since we have no more need for worry, we can replace our worries with worship. We can sing songs of praise to God like David:

For why would we fear? We are pursued by Your faithful protection and loving provision, everywhere, every day. So we draw near to You, God. (Inspired by Psalm 23:6)

When we focus on faith instead of fear, then God fills us with His hope. It's an even better deal than getting the "free refills for life" cup at Six Flags! When I was in high school, Power Balance bracelets were big. Supposedly these simple silicone bracelets with metal stickers improved your balance, strength, flexibility, and basically turn you into Superman.

One of my track teammates believed in her bracelet wholeheartedly. She wore her bracelet all day, every day; she believed that she needed her bracelet to win. However, all jewelry was banned during races. Sometimes, if the track officials were in a hurry or were lazy, she would get away with wearing her bracelet during a race. When she won, she would credit her win to her bracelet.

Other times, though, the officials would threaten that she take it off or be disqualified. It was in these times that she would worry. She would consider sitting out on the race. She *needed* her bracelet. Then my coach would console her and tell her that if she really believed, she could press the metal part of her bracelet onto her arm really hard and some of the power from the bracelet would be transferred into her, just enough power to run her race.

Luckily, God never limits His power when it comes to helping us. We never have to worry about whether we will win our race. We never have to worry about our future because it has already been written and can be found in Revelation.

Spoiler alert: God wins.

Everything will be okay.

So let's press on and live with integrity.

With the popularity and availability of music through iTunes, Amazon, Spotify, and Pandora, songs are becoming extremely accessible and universal. Yet when I browse through "Today's Top Hits" playlists, it is becoming harder and harder to find songs that aren't explicit. My teenage brother and I joke about our younger brother's love for Kidz Bop, but frankly I am glad that he is only exposed to edited versions of songs.

Because just like what goes up must come down, what goes in eventually comes out. Everything that we subject our minds to marinates, like spices flavoring meat. "A person full of goodness in his heart produces good things; a person with an evil reservoir in his heart pours out evil things. The heart overflows in the words a person speaks; your words reveal what's within your heart" (Luke 6:45 The Voice).

Watching rated-R movies doesn't make you a bad person. Listening to Drake doesn't make you a bad person. I like movies! I like Drake! But I do know that inappropriate movies and explicit songs are like that old psychology experiment about not thinking about pink elephants. When I watch movies and shows with sex and listen to music about sex, it becomes really hard to suppress my thoughts and not think about sex! Purity gets thrown to the back burner.

My favorite teacher in high school used to remind us every day that *words are important because words mean things*. Our words are powerful; they can be used as weapons, or tools, to further God's kingdom. "The weapons of the war we're fighting are not of this world but are powered by God and effective at tearing down the strongholds *erected against His truth*" (2 Corinthians 10:4 The Voice). "The tools of our trade aren't for marketing or manipulation; they are for demolishing that entire massively corrupt culture. We use our powerful God-tools for smashing warped philosophies, tearing down barriers erected against the truth of God, fitting every loose thought and emotion and impulse into the structure of life shaped by Christ. Our tools are ready at hand for clearing the ground of every obstruction and building lives of obedience into maturity" (2 Corinthians 10:5 MSG).

"Summing it all up, friends, I'd say you'll do best by filling your minds and meditating on things true, noble, reputable, authentic, compelling, gracious—the best, not the worst; the beautiful, not the ugly; things to praise, not things to curse. Put into practice what you learned from me, what you heard and saw and realized. Do that, and God, who makes everything work together, will work you into his most excellent harmonies" (Philippians 4:8–9 MSG).

Let's make the most out of our lives.

Fight the good fight.

Get ready for heaven.

In high school, we were required to perform a word study, and I chose to do mine on the German word *fernweh*. Unlike *wanderlust*, the popular American word meaning the desire to travel, *fernweh* elevates the urge to leave to a need. It is like the opposite of homesickness; it is the yearning to leave, to go, to belong elsewhere.

I think all Christians suffer from *fernweh*. We are not of this world, just like this war that we are fighting. We belong elsewhere, in heaven. We are all like Captain Jack Sparrow who mutters these beautiful words at the end of the fifth *Pirates* film:
"I have a rendezvous beyond my beloved horizon."

Verses for Thought

"And forgive us our debts,
as we also have forgiven our debtors.
And lead us not into temptation,
but deliver us from evil.
For if you forgive others their trespasses, your heavenly Father will also forgive you, but if you do not forgive others their trespasses, neither will your Father forgive your trespasses." (Matthew 6:12–15 ESV)

Reflection Questions

Is there anyone who you need to forgive?

Are there any negative influences in your life that are hindering your faith?

What steps can you take to limit or remove them?

Let Us Pray

Good, good Father,
Forgive me for all that I have done.
Thank You for Your compassion. Your love is where
I need to be.
Help me to give grace this week.
Help me to forgive, Father.
I fix my eyes on You, Lord, and dwell in Your truth.
Amen.

14

Treat Yo' Self

Resilience because of consequences from finances

We live in a "Treat Yo' Self" world.

Yasss girl, you deserve to look and feel good!

You just got paid; treat yo' self.

What would Tom Haverford do?

The world says that currency is key. But what does Jesus say? "You can't worship two gods at once. *Loving* one god, you'll end up hating the other. Adoration of one feeds contempt for the other. You can't worship God and Money both" (Matthew 6:24 MSG).

I am the poster child of the prodigal son. I chose the wrong god to worship and was left empty. But I ultimately belong to a God who forgives and restores when I come to Him with an open, apologetic heart. By losing everything, God has taught me not just the value of money, but how it can be used as a vessel for His goodness and grace.

It has been misquoted too many times that the Bible says "money is the root of all evil"—that is only half of the verse! The Bible actually says, "For the love of money is the root of all evil" (1 Timothy 6:10a KJV). Corruption and compulsion toward consumption are issues that stem from the heart. Money, itself, is not the problem.

Everyone uses currency; all cultures have their own variation of it. Money establishes worth and warrants connection. Currency has been an integration of every civilization throughout history, so it is no wonder why Jesus talked about it so much. He knew that money was a hot topic that constantly consumed the minds of His audiences. So Jesus gave this reminder:

> Don't reduce your life to the pursuit of food and drink; don't let your mind be filled with anxiety. People of the world who don't know God pursue these things, *but you have a Father caring for you,* a Father who knows all your needs. Since you don't need to worry—about security and safety, about food and clothing—then pursue God's kingdom first and foremost, and these other things will come to you as well … That means you can sell your possessions and give generously to the poor. You can have a different kind of savings plan: one that never depreciates, one that never defaults, one that can't be plundered by crooks or destroyed by natural calamities. (Luke 12:29–31, 33 The Voice)

Jesus was not worried about His believers' budgets. He knew where their funding was coming from—not from their employers or their endeavors, but from God. Instead of focusing on possessions and payments, Jesus made the focal point the power of the heart and its desires.

> Is there anyone here who, planning to build a new house, doesn't first sit down and figure the cost so you'll know if you can complete it? If you only get the foundation laid and then run out of money, you're going to look pretty foolish. Everyone passing by will poke fun at you: "He started something he couldn't finish." Simply put, if you're not willing to take what is dearest to you,

whether plans or people, and kiss it good-bye, you
can't be my disciple. (Luke 14:28–30, 33 MSG)

Jesus loved the poor and spent a lot of time among those who
had little. "Blessed are you who are poor, for yours is the kingdom
of God," He said (Luke 6:20b ESV). Sometimes, when you have
only a little, then it becomes easier to see what is important.
Likewise, sometimes, when you have a lot, it becomes harder to
let go. Jesus saw this continually during tithe time in the temple.

Jesus looked up and saw rich men putting their
money into the money box in the house of God.
He saw a poor woman whose husband had died.
She put in two very small pieces of money. He
said, "I tell you the truth, this poor woman has
put in more than all of them. For they have put
in a little of the money they had no need for. She
is very poor and has put in all she had. She has
put in what she needed for her own living." (Luke
21:1–4 NLV)

Tithing can be a difficult thing. It can often be an awkward
part of church services. Tithing used to be a requirement of the
Old Testament law. However, it didn't start out that way. The
tradition of tithing began when Jacob, son of Abraham's Isaac,
received a visit from God in a dream. God promised to be Jacob's
provision, so Jacob's heart's response was to willingly give back
10 percent of everything he was provided with. He chose to give
(see Genesis 28:22).

The widow in the temple stretched her faith with her giving,
for she knew that she would be okay. She believed that if she
surrendered everything, that her God would deliver and be her
provision. Jesus laid out His expectations again for a rich, young
ruler.

And as [Jesus] was setting out on his journey, a man ran up and knelt before him and asked him, "Good Teacher, what must I do to inherit eternal life?"

And Jesus said to him, "Why do you call me good? No one is good except God alone. You know the commandments: 'Do not murder, Do not commit adultery, Do not steal, Do not bear false witness, Do not defraud, Honor your father and mother.'"

And he said to him, "Teacher, all these I have kept from my youth."

And Jesus, looking at him, loved him, and said to him, "You lack one thing: go, sell all that you have and give to the poor, and you will have treasure in heaven; and come, follow me." Disheartened by the saying, he went away sorrowful, for he had great possessions. And Jesus looked around and said to his disciples, "How difficult it will be for those who have wealth to enter the kingdom of God!" And the disciples were amazed at his words. But Jesus said to them again, "Children, how difficult it is to enter the kingdom of God! It is easier for a camel to go through the eye of a needle than for a rich person to enter the kingdom of God."

And they were exceedingly astonished, and said to him, "Then who can be saved?"

Jesus looked at them and said, "With man it is impossible, but not with God. For all things are possible with God." (Mark 10:17–27 ESV)

Jesus doesn't exclude rich people from receiving blessing, but He knows how difficult it can be for them to live with abandon.

Letting go is hard when you are young.

Letting go is hard when you are rich.

Letting go is hard when you are rulers or in high authority.

Letting go is hard, but it is *not* impossible.

How we treat our belongings is a direct indicator of what is in our hearts. When we do not share our riches—when we store them away and keep them to ourselves—then we are not sharing the characteristics with Jesus that He said were results of faith. If we truly believe in the goodness of God, then we should be spreading His love and His provision with the rest of His beloved creation.

God likes using people with riches. There were several wealthy women who were a part of the group that followed Jesus throughout His ministry. These devoted women, women like Mary Magdalene, Susanna, and Joanna, used their own money to provide for Jesus and His disciples. These women were vital to His operation.

The amount of money that you have has no indication of the amount of worth that God sees in you. He created all of us. We are His children. When the Israelites, God's chosen people, were wandering in the desert, God supplied their every need. He provided safety in travel, success in battle, and sustenance for survival.

Yet, the Israelites were very grumpy people. Although God delivered them from slavery in Egypt and personally led them through the desert toward the land of milk and honey, they complained every step of the way. Sometimes I become so embittered while reading the book of Exodus, until I realize that I am frustrated because I see so much of myself in the Israelites. When difficult things come my way, I fall on the floor and throw a temper tantrum, completely forgetting about who holds my hand and has taken care of me every step of the way.

God split the Red Sea when His people were threatened, and He will do it again.

God provided water when His people were thirsty, and He will do it again.

God provided food when His people were hungry, and He will do it again.

But notice that God doesn't operate like Oprah does. He doesn't just ante up wins in Vegas. He doesn't leisurely liquidate via lottery tickets. He gives a daily portion.

When God provided aliment to the Israelites, He did so with manna: a new, thin, flaky bread. He left His people with this instruction:

> "Gather only as much of it as you should eat by yourself. Pick up two quarts *of bread* for each person who lives in your tent."
>
> The Israelites did as they were told. Some people gathered a lot, others gathered less. When they used a two-quart jar to measure it, the one who had gathered a lot didn't have more than he needed; and the one who gathered less had just what he needed. *Miraculously,* each person *and each family*—regardless of how much they gathered—had exactly what they needed. (Exodus 16:16b–18 The Voice)

Everyone has needs. Jesus already established that we don't need to worry about our own needs, about food and drink and clothing. When we look at our needs through a lens of anxiety, then our judgments and decisions become blurry. Jacob's big brother, Esau, once saw his hunger through a lens of anxiety, and it caused him to make a rash decision.

> Esau *(to Jacob)*: Please let me have some of that red stew you have there. I'm famished! (That's why he was nicknamed Edom, *which means "red."*)

> Jacob sees Esau's weakness and decides to take advantage of the situation.
> Jacob: First, you have to sell me your birthright.
> Esau: Look! I am about to die *of starvation!* What good is my birthright to me *if I am dead?*
> Jacob: Swear to me first!
> And so Esau swore to Jacob and handed over his rights as the firstborn son. Then Jacob gave Esau some bread and lentil stew. Esau ate and drank. When he was satisfied, Esau went his way *as if nothing had happened.* Esau treated his valuable birthright contemptuously. (Genesis 25:30–34 The Voice)

Esau put his own needs first. Jacob put his own needs first.

What if … what if we put others' needs first?

What if we were generous with others instead of just ourselves?

What if we let God go crazy through us?

What if we let Him change a life through what He's given us?

Winston Churchill said that "we make a living by what we get, but we make a life by what we give." The Bible says that "a giving person will receive much *in return,* and someone who gives water will also receive the water *he needs*" (Proverbs 11:25 The Voice). Generosity puts God's provisions into circulation. His economy is established through sharing. Shifting the spotlight from getting to giving and stepping into a God-reality will break chains of anxiety, of hopelessness, of fear.

Money is a vessel.

A vessel of worship.

A vessel of gratefulness.

A vessel of love.

A vessel administered through giving.

The goal of a giver should be to offer up the overflow of the heart—"otherwise, you've reluctantly grumbled 'yes' because you felt you had to or because you couldn't say 'no,' *but this isn't the way God wants it.* For *we know that* 'God loves a cheerful giver.' God is ready to overwhelm you with more blessings than you could ever imagine so that you'll always be taken care of in every way and you'll have more than enough to share" (2 Corinthians 9:7b–8 The Voice).

God blessed His humble servant Abraham when He obeyed, and in return, Abraham blessed those around him. In this way, people saw that Abe was honest and fair and knew that He was favored by God. God got the glory through the giving.

Jesus's cousin, John the Baptist, was another godly giver. He had a simple philosophy:

> The person who has two shirts must share with the person who has none. And the person with food must share with the one in need. (Luke 3:11 The Voice)

I don't know about you, but I have a lot of shirts. I have workout shirts, work shirts, dress shirts, summer shirts, winter shirts, shirts with elephants on them, shirts with spaghetti straps, shirts with pompoms, you name it. But do I need all of them? Definitely not. There are kids out there who have *no* shirts.

City streets are full of homeless, hungry people. Yet, how often, as we go about our days, do we step around the sinners, the broken, the hurting, as if they deserve to be there; *as if we are not exactly like them.* We are the church. We should be the Good Samaritans, the ones with compassion and mercy, because compassion and mercy have been poured unto us.

The community of the first Christians figured out how to become like that. They committed themselves to living like the disciples instructed. They continually gathered together to break bread for fellowship and prayer. "There was an intense sense of togetherness among all who believed; they shared all their material possessions in trust. They sold any possessions and goods *that did not benefit the community* and used the money to help everyone in need ... *During those days,* the entire community of believers was deeply united in heart and soul to such an extent that they stopped claiming private ownership of their possessions. Instead, they held everything in common. The apostles with great power gave their eyewitness reports of the resurrection of the Lord Jesus. Everyone was surrounded by an extraordinary grace. Not a single person in the community was in need because those who had been affluent sold their houses or lands and brought the proceeds to the emissaries of the Lord. They then distributed the funds to individuals according to their needs" (Acts 2:44–45, 4:32–35 The Voice).

This may seem like an unobtainable society. But I can assure you that it isn't! It all begins and ends with the heart. We need only to be still, listen, and trust that God is in control.

Verses for Thought

> "If you want to be extraordinary—love your enemies! Do good *without restraint!* Lend *with abandon!* Don't expect anything in return! Then you'll receive the truly great reward—you will be children of the Most High—for God is kind to the ungrateful and those who are wicked … Don't hold back—give freely, and you'll have plenty poured back into your lap—a good measure, pressed down, shaken together, brimming over. You'll receive in the same measure you give." (Luke 6:35, 38 The Voice)

Reflection Question

Where does your heart lie? Which god are you worshipping—God or money?

What do you base your budget on?

Do you tithe regularly?

Let Us Pray

> *God,*
> *Like Jacob, I dedicate ten percent of all that You give me as a gift back to You*
> *As a token of my gratitude.*
> *Help me to be a great giver.*
> *Break my heart for what breaks Yours, God.*
> *Amen.*

15

With Us

Resilience because of consequences from relationships

I hate Christmas music. I don't hate the message, just the incessant repetition. Whether at work, in the car, doing Christmas shopping, or watching Christmas movies, the same songs are played over and over. Some stores these days begin playing the tunes in July! We get it, Santa baby. You will be home for a jingle-bell-rockin'-around-the-Christmas-tree-how-lovely-are-your-branches white Christmas. Good grief, Charlie Brown!

With the holidays also comes the familiar feeling of loneliness. Although Christmas may be the most wonderful time of the year for some, it also can be the loneliest time of the year for many. Mother Teresa once said, "I have come to realize more and more that the greatest disease and the greatest suffering is to be unwanted, unloved, uncared for, to be shunned by everybody, to be just nobody to anybody." Powerful, yeah?

While independence and self-sufficiency are good, fellowship and community are good, too. God did not stop after He created Adam. He then made Eve. God invented companionship because it is not good to be alone (see Genesis 2:18).

I have been single my entire life. I used to crave having a boyfriend. I would juxtapose my name with the last name of each of my crushes, whether celebrity or in my reality. I would hit on guys myself and ask *them* out, thinking that would get me somewhere (and ladies, no, it doesn't! One of my favorite authors, Karen Kingsbury, often repeats this line about relationships in many of her books: "The next time that boy pursues you, he better do it like a dying man looking for water in a desert. When it's the right guy, you'll know, because he'll cherish you." He will be worth the wait.).

But when I looked back on my relentless pursuit for love and belonging, the only thing that I saw was the word that I used to begin every sentence in that last paragraph: *I*. I was so self-absorbed in my failures in relationships. I began to realize what I brought to the table—selfishness, bitterness, impatience—and I became unafraid to sit alone. I gave up and indulged in meals for two by myself. *Apparently I'm supposed to be alone, so why bother?*

The devil loves when we are alone. We are vulnerable, and our minds become pliable, able to bend this way and that as we reason and debate major life choices. Have you ever noticed that in movies when they show the little devil and the little angel arguing on each shoulder that the main character is always isolated? If the enemy can steal our full attention, then he will do everything in his power to steal more than that: our vision, our motivation, our dedication.

Although loneliness can seem like the worst feeling in the world, it can act as an invitation to draw near to God. I frequently feel lonely at nighttime, when I cannot sleep and the weight of the world whirls around in my mind, creating chaos like the tornado in *The Wizard of Oz*. But then I remember the beautiful chorus to Laura Story's song "Blessings":

> 'Cause what if Your blessings come through raindrops
> What if Your healing comes through tears?
> What if a thousand sleepless nights
> Are what it takes to know You're near?

Friend, you may feel lonely, but you are never alone. One of *Merriam-Webster*'s definitions for "lonely" is "not frequented by human beings." On days when my friends are too busy to hang and on nights when I am in my room by myself, I often feel a tug at my heart and hear God whisper: "This is a time for you and Me. Draw near to Me, and I will draw near to you" (see James 4:8).

When I accept God's invitation, and I bring my needs to Him instead of to people, He meets and exceeds those needs. My feeling of loneliness dissipates. I find the time that I am frequented by human beings as precious and enjoyable despite the disappointment that they sometimes bring, because I place my expectations and value in the time when I am frequented by a heavenly being.

Logging in to social media and latching on to humans will always disappoint if they are sought out with the intent of finding the affirmation that only God can provide. Committing to a romantic relationship and clinging to a partner will always disappoint if they are sought out with the intent of finding the affirmation that only God can provide.

Draw near to Me, and I will draw near to you.

Then you will begin to notice that God will bring two types of people into your life. The first group of people are those who will help you strengthen your relationship with God. Community is a communication vessel to point us toward Jesus and not away from Him. But the first step to finding these people is to get connected.

Join a small group.

Find a mentor.

Meet with an elder at your church.

The second group of people are those who *you* will help strengthen in *their* relationship with God. The crazy thing about these particular people is that most of the time, you will not even recognize them or the fact that you are affecting them. The only steps are to listen and be willing. God will do the prompting and the directing. His commands will sound something like:

Smile at the lady walking past you.
Tell the person visiting your church your story.
Take that person out to lunch.

Sometimes your stories will align, and you will find out that you have mutual friends on Facebook, and you walk away hand in hand singing "It's a Small World (After All)" Other times, you will not learn the reasoning behind your encounters until you get to heaven, but I think that is part of what it makes it so exciting.

Remember back in chapter three when Jesus said, "'Love the Lord your God with all your passion and prayer and intelligence.' This is the most important, the first on any list. But there is a second to set alongside it: 'Love others as well as you love yourself.' These two commands are pegs; everything in God's Law and the Prophets hangs from them" (Matthew 22:37–40 MSG). It is the same principle that we have established here:

1. Love when you are frequented by your heavenly being.
2. Love when you are frequented by human beings.

Notice how Jesus says to love others *as well as you love yourself.* It is vital to love yourself so that you can love others. You cannot pour from an empty cup. You cannot help and give without being willing to be filled first.

Draw near to Me, and I will draw near to you.

No one is a better example of all these fundamentals than Jesus Himself. Oh, how I love Him! He spoke so intentionally and fervidly that everything is still just as applicable and personal today, a mere two thousand years later! Is not it also so great that we serve a God who does not just bark out all these orders, but who actually became a man and lived them out Himself? It is beautiful; so, so beautiful.

"What a Beautiful Name It Is"

Although I abhor Christmas songs, I will never tire of the Christmas story. I hear it during the traditional viewings of *A Charlie Brown Christmas* and during my little brother's Christmas plays. Amid the magic and the imagery and the manger, my favorite part of the story is when Jesus's name is revealed:

> Behold, the virgin shall conceive and bear a son,
> and they shall call his name Immanuel
> (which means "God with us").
> (Isaiah 7:14b; Matthew 1:23 ESV)

The most awesome part is that this reveal, *these exact words*, were uttered years and years before the birth of Jesus by a man who would never even meet Him. Yet, he believed in the meaning behind the name Immanuel, *God with us*. This very concept makes me feel so giddy and want to sing out the lyrics to some of my favorite songs:

"*What a beautiful name it is!*"[1]

"*And isn't the name of Jesus all we need?*"[2]

Oh yes, Lord, it is.

So once our little baby was born and officially received His full name—Jesus Christ Immanuel Lord Son of God Hyphen Also Son of Mary and Joseph—He grew. "And Jesus kept on growing—in wisdom, in physical stature, in favor with God, and in favor with others" (Luke 2:52 The Voice).

Jesus's ministry didn't begin until He was about thirty years old (see Luke 3:23). *Thirty years old!* He did not just drop down here to earth and begin preaching as an already grown and intelligent man. How creepy would that have been? No, instead He lived, He learned, and He loved until His time came. Jesus's time on earth

---

[1] "What a Beautiful Name," Hillsong Worship
[2] "Isn't the Name," Bethany Worship

was not all serious and political. He celebrated in the city, studied in the synagogue, and connected with community. I love the way that Pastor Brian Houston puts it:

> Living fully, loving completely, leading boldly—these are the hallmarks of Jesus' time on earth. Whether you're taking baby steps or giant strides, walking on water or running on empty, wherever you are in your journey of faith, Jesus is the ultimate guide and companion. Jesus lived fully present in each moment every day. He gave His attention, His heart, and His energy to those around Him who needed Him even as He advanced God's kingdom in the most dramatic way possible. He alone provides us with a model of a big, wide-open life fully lived.

"Jesus Wept"

Growing up in a Christian school, I was required to learn a new memory verse every Monday and then was tested on said verse the following Friday. It was always my least favorite part of the week because my memory was not my strong suit. But I became excited when my friends taught me the shortest verse in the Bible, "Jesus wept," and from that day on, I joined in on their futile weekly petitions to substitute our preassigned memory verses to the shortest verse in the Bible (see John 11:35).

It wasn't until I was much older that I learned the context of this mysterious verse. *Why is Jesus crying?* I would wonder. *Isn't He my Savior? My strong tower? The One who collects my tears?* (see Psalm 56:8). But then I read the full story.

Jesus was friends with a trio of siblings named Mary, Martha, and Lazarus from the town of Bethany. Now, Lazarus became gravely ill, so his sisters sent word to Jesus. It makes sense. Jesus is their friend. He is also the great healer. In previous occasions like this, Jesus would typically go to the sick, say because of your faith you are healed, and then everyone goes away celebrating. But this time, He does something different.

Jesus heard the message.

> Jesus: His sickness will not end in his death but will bring great glory to God. As these events unfold, the Son of God will be exalted.
> Jesus *dearly* loved Mary, Martha, and Lazarus. However, after receiving this news, He waited two more days where He was. (John 11:4–6 The Voice)

Then, Jesus made His way to Bethany. By the time that He had arrived, Lazarus was dead and buried. Jesus-the-Miraculous-Healer-and-Savior-Say-What? Did not Jesus *just* say that Lazarus's sickness will not end in his death?
He did, and it didn't.
That was not the end.
Jesus asked to see Mary and Martha.

Mary approached Jesus, saw Him, and fell at His feet.

> Mary: Lord, if only You had been here, my brother would still be alive.
> When Jesus saw Mary's *profound grief and the moaning and* weeping of her companions, He was deeply moved *by their pain* in His spirit and was intensely troubled.
> Jesus: Where have you laid his body?
> Jews: Come and see, Lord.

As they walked, Jesus wept; and everyone
noticed how much Jesus must have loved Lazarus.
(John 11:32–35 The Voice)

How beautiful is that? He wept with Mary and Martha about Lazarus. Jesus showed up. He loved. He embodied what would later be Paul's instruction to "rejoice with those who rejoice, weep with those who weep" (Romans 12:15 ESV). Then, once Jesus, Mary, and Martha wiped one another's tears and consoled with comforting hugs, Jesus "called out in a thunderous voice. 'Lazarus, come out!'" (John 11:43b The Voice).

Once again, the Lord's voice drew out life. Jesus raised His friend up and out of his grave only days before Jesus would be placed in His own grave. Jesus lived deliberately and loved intentionally with His sole goal of fulfilling His Father's will—a will that benefitted our well-being over Jesus's. That's the premise of our faith: He loved us so that we could love. This love is a crazy, unconditional love that chooses compassion over comfort or convenience. Jesus's love longed to lure people into the next life. With heaven in clear sight, there is so much more purpose in this life.

Drag Them In

My family holds this competition every summer when we go camping at our favorite lake. The competition takes place on a giant inflatable trampoline right out on the water. The rules are simple. Everyone must stand up without holding one another or the trampoline and then must balance amid the waves and the weight of everyone else. Whoever touches the trampoline or falls into the water first loses. This is the most serious and anticipated event of the year for my family. People strategize and trash talk, saying, "If I'm going down, you are coming down with me."

That is what the passion for finding fellow Christ followers should sound like! "If I'm going to heaven, you are coming to heaven with me." It's aggressive, but fun. When I used to hear pastors say that I should be inviting more people to church, I used to shake it off. Being vulnerable and offering an invitation only to be answered with rejection just didn't sound like fun to me. But then someone reminded me of one of Jesus's parables:

> For there was once a man who threw a great dinner party and invited many. When it was time for dinner, he sent out his servant to the invited guests, saying, "Come on in; the food's on the table."
>
> Then they all began to beg off, one after another making excuses. The first said, "I bought a piece of property and need to look it over. Send my regrets."
>
> Another said, "I just bought five teams of oxen, and I really need to check them out. Send my regrets."
>
> And yet another said, "I just got married and need to get home to my wife."
>
> The servant went back and told the master what had happened. He was outraged and told the servant, "Quickly, get out into the city streets and alleys. Collect all who look like they need a square meal, all the misfits and homeless and wretched you can lay your hands on, and bring them here."
>
> The servant reported back, "Master, I did what you commanded—and there's still room."
>
> The master said, "Then go to the country roads. Whoever you find, drag them in. I want my house full! Let me tell you, not one of those originally invited is going to get so much as a bite at my dinner party." (Luke 14:16b–24 MSG)

What do you think would happen if we were so enthusiastic, so passionate, so persistent that we began to *gracefully* drag people into church? There would be a revival! There would be hope! Jesus wants us to see just how the kingdom of God works and who will be in it. Not the proud and the privileged who puff themselves up, but the misfits and the homeless and the wretched *because they are still deserving.*

First Is the Worst

When my brother and I were younger, we would always race around and then tease each other by chanting, "First is the worst, second is the best, third is the one with the hairy chest!" In hindsight, I am not even sure why we used to say that because

1) ew, that's gross!
2) there were only two of us …
3) isn't the whole point of racing to win? To finish first?

Well, according to Jesus, no! It isn't!

> Jesus: Many of those who are the first will be last, and those who are the last will be first. The kingdom of heaven is like a wealthy landowner who got up early in the morning and went out, first thing, to hire workers to tend his vineyard. He agreed to pay them a day's wage for the day's work. The workers headed to the vineyard *while the landowner headed home to deal with some paperwork.* About three hours later, he went back to the marketplace. He saw *some unemployed* men standing around with nothing to do.

Landowner: *Do you need some work?* Go over to my vineyard *and join the crew there.* I'll pay you well.

So off they went *to join the crew at the vineyard.* About three hours later, and then three hours after that, *the landowner went back to the market and saw another crew of men and hired them, too, sending them off to his vineyard and promising to pay them well.* Then finally late in the afternoon, *at the cusp of night,* the landowner walked again through *the marketplace,* and he saw other *workers* still standing around.

Landowner: Why have you been standing here all day, doing nothing?

Workers: Because no one has hired us.

Landowner: Well, you should go over to my vineyard *and work.*

And off the workers went. When quitting time arrived, the landowner called to his foreman.

Landowner: Pay the workers their day's wages, beginning with the workers I hired most recently and ending with the workers who have been here all day.

So the workers who had been hired just a short while before came to the foreman, and he paid them each a day's wage. *Then other workers who had arrived during the day were paid, each of them a day's wage.* Finally, the workers who'd been toiling since early morning came thinking they'd be paid more, but the foreman paid each of them a day's wage. As they received their pay, this last group of workers began to protest.

First Workers: *We've been here since the crack of dawn!* And you're paying us the exact same wage you paid the crew that just showed up. *We deserve more than they do.* We've been slogging in the heat of the sun all day—*these others haven't worked nearly as long as we have!*

The landowner heard these protests.

Landowner *(to a worker)*: Friend, no one has been wronged here today. *This isn't about what you deserve.* You agreed to work for a day's wage, did you not?

So take your money and go home. *I can give my money to whomever I please, and* it pleases me to pay everyone the same amount of money. Do you think I don't have the right to dispose of my money as I wish? Or does my generosity somehow prick at you?

And that is your picture: The last will be first and the first will be last. (Matthew 19:30, 20:1–16 The Voice)

Again, Jesus was trying to paint us a picture of the precedents of the kingdom of God. Fairness is not the same in His eyes as it is ours. The kingdom of God is not built on numbers or measured in time. It is not about who followed God first or who served the most. Jesus cares about the people. He wants His house full! He wants everyone to receive!

With Us

Jesus did not become a man and die just because He needed us—He came to be *with us.* Jesus showed us how to love radically and live earth-shaking, eternal-worshipping, everlasting lives!

Through Him we find our needs met, our identities restored, and our dreams empowered.

Although Jesus, the Son of Man, has long since ascended into heaven, He has not left us here alone. Before His departure, Jesus promised, "I will talk to the Father, and he'll provide you another Friend so that you will always have someone with you. This Friend is the Spirit of Truth. The godless world can't take him in because it doesn't have eyes to see him, doesn't know what to look for. But you know him already because he has been staying with you, and will even be in you!" (John 14:16–17 MSG).

The spirit of truth—the Holy Spirit—was with God in the beginning when He said, "Let us make human beings in our image, make them reflecting our nature" (Genesis 1:26a MSG). Just as we crave companionship, the Holy Spirit's greatest desire is to be our closest friend.

So let us strive to not just live *for* God, but to live with Him.

Verse for Thought

"I can do all things with the help of Christ, who strengthens me." (Philippians 4:13 NMB)

Reflection Questions

What is your favorite name of Jesus? Why?

Who do you need to love with a love like Jesus?

How can you do that? With rejoicing as they rejoice, or with mourning as they mourn?

Who can you invite to church this week?

Who do you need to serve this week by stepping back and putting them first?

Let Us Pray

> *God,*
> *Thank You for becoming God with us in Bethlehem.*
> *Thank You for becoming God for us on the cross.*
> *Thank You for becoming God in us during the Pentecost.*
> *I welcome You in.*
> *Fill me with Your presence, with Your Holy Spirit.*
> *Without You, I struggle,*

but with You, *we are unstoppable.*
I take courage as You take control.
You are the way;
All things take life and shape and purpose through You.
You are almighty, all knowing, all-consuming, and worthy of all praise, God.
Amen.

16

Let Us Pray

Resilience because of consequences from prayer

When I was a little girl, my mom passed down her childhood dollhouse to me. It was homemade; carefully handcrafted out of wood by my grandfather. Every day, to my delight, my imagination would engage, and my little dolls would come to life and join me for tea time, soccer games, and pool parties.

As I grew up and learned more about who God was, is, and is to come, I began to think of Him and this universe as the God with His dollhouse. His dollhouse is carefully handcrafted by voice—His voice. Every day, to His delight, His breath of life engages, and He watches as His little children come alive and join Him in worship, in prayer, and in fasting.

Just like I used to carefully choose each of my doll's outfits and uniquely assign each doll with a name, favorite color, daily routine, and love-life status, I believe that God takes pride in each of our own distinct and unique characteristics. I believe that God cares about the big things, or the milestones, like where you go to school, and who you marry, and what job you get. I believe that He also cares about the little things, like who wins each soccer game and your favorite food. Do you know why? Because He cares about *you*. He created *you*.

And everything—every little tiny detail—ultimately points back to Him, giving God the glory. It's similar to how they teach you to write essays in school: every sentence should be a reflection or a proof of the thesis statement, right? Well, God is the thesis statement of the world.

So why do we insist so fervently on being independent and neglecting to live life with Him? Maybe we don't mean to. But we are given the opportunity to have direct communication with Him, and most people only take advantage of this generous correspondence opportunity at bedtime, before meals, or during an emergency.

Our souls naturally thirst for God. Just as our physical bodies thirst for water daily lest they become dehydrated and begin to deplete, our souls also require spiritual water to avoid this same fate. Jesus once offered a woman at a well this very water that He offers to us today: "I offer water that will become a wellspring within you that gives life throughout eternity. You will never be thirsty again" (John 4:14 The Voice). Of course, Jesus was offering more than just pure liquid hydrogen and oxygen. He was offering more than just religion. He was offering a relationship, and any good relationship requires communication.

I admit, my current prayer life is lacking. Sure, I can recite catchy rhymes before I eat, just like my teachers instructed me to do in elementary school.

> *God is great!*
> *God is good!*
> *Let us thank Him*
> *For our food.*
> *Amen.*

I can recite the Lord's Prayer before bedtime, too:

> *Our Father in heaven,*
> *Hallowed be Your name.*
> *Your kingdom come.*
> *Your will be done*

On earth as it is in heaven.
Give us day by day our daily bread.
And forgive us our sins,
For we also forgive everyone who is indebted to us.
And do not lead us into temptation,
But deliver us from the evil one. (Luke 11:2b–4
NKJV)

But eventually, these echoed phrases begin to morph from meaningful maxims into mere mutterings. Christians can communicate with God because of Jesus's gift of the Holy Spirit. The Holy Spirit dwells in us. He doesn't just wait for us at the dinner table or at our bedsides. He goes with us everywhere. He is omnipresent. How cool is that? So why don't we include Him all throughout our days? That is all that prayer needs to be! Simply including God in our thoughts. After all, He already knows what we are thinking.

O Eternal One, You have explored my heart and
know exactly who I am;
   You even know the small details like when I
take a seat and when I stand up
      again.
   Even when I am far away, You know what I'm
thinking.
   You observe my wanderings and my sleeping,
my waking and my dreaming,
   and You know everything I do in more detail
than even I know.
   You know what I'm going to say long before I
say it.
   It is true, Eternal One, that You know everything
and everyone. (Psalm 139:1–4 The Voice)

God longs to be included, to be acknowledged by His children in His dollhouse. He desires to assuage our anger, comfort our cries, placate our pain, and cease our grief. God takes joy in hearing our joy.

King David is one of my favorite Bible dudes. David was confident that he could defeat the giant Goliath. How? His certainty stemmed from his faith in God, which was constantly stirred and strengthened by their fellowship. Speaker and best-selling author Angie Smith says about him, "David wasn't a man after God's own heart because he didn't sin; he was a man after God's own heart because He kept coming back to God." There is power in persistent prayer (see Micah 7:7).

So pray before you plan. Pray instead of puzzle about your problems (see Philippians 4:6). This is something that I have to actively work on all of the time. Praying continually (see 1 Thessalonians 5:17). Generating a tendency to pray instead of to text. Praying about my ideas for work, my dreams for the future, my plans for my day, as much as I think about them.

Prayer is not a scary thing. Eloquence is not a prerequisite. Your prayer doesn't need to be fluent or follow a formula. Silence, stillness, screams, shouts, scriptures, and songs are all beautiful and acceptable forms of worship in the right settings. I love author Max Lucado's take on prayer: "Our prayers may be awkward. Our attempts may be feeble. But since the power of prayer is in the One who hears it and not in the one who says it, our prayers do make a difference." Reverence and honesty are the principals of prayer.

Setting can be essential as well. Many people go to church to pray. Rightly so, as the house of God is a great place for prayer. But so is your house, a car, the shower, your workplace, a park, the post office. Jesus often wandered into the wilderness to pray (see Luke 5:16).

If you are a beginner pray-er, find your secret place. Schedule a date between yourself and God. Then start! If you don't know where to even begin, chase the rabbit. Start to pray. Tell God about your day or about your feelings or describe your setting. If your mind wanders, then pray about what your mind wanders to. Don't fret over the rabbit trails. My mom told me long ago that the way to pray is to talk to God like you would talk to a friend, and that has stuck with me ever since. The apostle Paul said that "I\if we don't know how or what to pray, it doesn't matter. [God] does our praying in and for us, making prayer out of our wordless sighs, our aching groans" (Romans 8:27 MSG).

Even Jesus said, *"Your prayers need not be labored or lengthy or grandiose*—for your Father knows what you need before you ever ask Him" (Matthew 6:8b The Voice). Jesus then proceeded to provide an example of how prayers can go. "Your prayers, rather, should be *simple,* like this ..." and then he launched into the Lord's Prayer (Matthew 6:9a The Voice). I think it is important to note that Jesus said "Like this." He wants us to make it our own. Deviate. Personalize it and make it sincere. It is merely a guide, a blueprint, for intentional prayer:

> Our Father in heaven,
> let Your name remain holy.
> Bring about Your kingdom.
> Manifest Your will here on earth,
> as it is manifest in heaven. (Matthew 6:9b–10 The Voice)

1. **Glorify Him**

Acknowledge how awesome God is. He is so worthy of all praise. Everything is for Him; this is His dollhouse, after all. It's more than thinking of reasons to thank Him; it's about praising God for His plan and purpose.

> *Give us each day that day's bread*—no more, no less. (Matthew 6:11 The Voice)

2. His Provision

Ask God to fulfill your needs and then trust that He will. Thank Him for His constant provision. What if you woke up tomorrow with only the things that you thanked Him for today?

> *And forgive us our debts as we forgive those who owe us something.* (Matthew 6:12 The Voice)

3. Forgive Me

When I ride the *Pirates of the Caribbean* ride at Disneyland, I never cease to point out a strange detail to the fellow passengers in my boat once we arrive in the last room. In this room is the classic scene where some pirate prisoners are trying to woo a dog with the keys to their cell door. If you take a close look at one of the cell walls, you can see that a fallen, fiery tree has broken open a way of escape (I may or may not have ridden this ride too many times …).

We all screw up in life. We are all surrounded by sin and shame. Although shame can serve as a prison, the doors to our cells has been broken open by Jesus. Through our confession and His forgiveness, we can walk out with the freedom of grace.

4. Forgive Them

Everyone deserves the chance to be freed from sin and shame. Salvation and forgiveness are both equal-opportunity entities. Holding on to anger and refusing to forgive someone is most likely hurting you more than it is the other person. In the wise words of Gautama Buddha, "Holding on to anger is like grasping a hot coal with the intent of throwing it at someone else; you are the one who gets burned." Instead, let go and let God.

Pray for those around you. Paul was always reminding people to do so. "I urge you, first of all, to pray for all people. ask God to help them; intercede on their behalf, and give thanks for them" (1 Timothy 2:1 NLT). If God answered all of your prayers, would they change the world or just yours? Praying for others does radical things. It reconstructs ruined relationships. Communication with God changes your attitude and then discharges the issue from your hands and places it in the hands of God—with whom, may I remind you, nothing is impossible. Positive praying trumps positive thinking and personal achieving.

> Lead us not into temptation,
> but deliver us from evil.
> [But let Your kingdom be,
> and let it be powerful and glorious forever. Amen.]
> (Matthew 6:13 The Voice)

5. Temptation

Life can become difficult at times. Jesus mentions that temptation is out there; evil is out there. But we can pray for God to help us and direct us toward safety. We do not always need to be so serious and focused on the potential danger. Paul instruct us as such: " *Do not forget to* rejoice, for hope is always just around the corner. Hold up through the hard times that are coming, and devote yourselves to prayer" (Romans 12:12 The Voice).

Intentional prayer is an expression of faith. The act of praying is the first step—for you can't expect to win the lottery without first purchasing a ticket—but you must also believe in what you pray for. Your heart has to back the words of your prayers. Time after time, Jesus placed emphasis on the power of the faith of those who He was healing. "Your faith has saved you," He would say (see Matthew 9:23; Mark 5:34; Luke 7:50, Luke 17:19). Jesus informed His disciples that if they had faith and did not doubt, then their faith could move mountains! The same is true to the mountainous problems in our lives. "And whatever you ask in prayer, you will receive, if you have faith" (Matthew 21:22 ESV). God stands by His promises. His answers may not match with our expectations, but they always complement our well-being and contribute to His overarching, perfect plan for our lives.

Verse for Thought

"Pray always. Pray in the Spirit. Pray about everything in every way you know how! And keeping all this in mind, pray on behalf of God's people. Keep on praying feverishly, and be on the lookout *until evil has been stayed.*" (Ephesians 6:18 The Voice)

Reflection Question

Prayer Blueprint:

Glorify Him: What is your favorite attribute of God?

His Provision: What are your essential needs? What has God done for you lately?

Forgive Me: What have you been struggling with lately?

Forgive Them: Who in your life do you need to extend grace to?

Temptation: In what area do you need to activate your faith? Are there any mountains in your life that need moving?

Let Us Pray

Practice! Write your own prayer this time. Use the blueprint above if you would like.

PART 3

Resilience in the Turbulence

17

Planted Passions

"Practically sleepwalking, scared for my life, and excited beyond belief, I am stepping off of the plane." That was my journal entry from my first solo international trip. I was eighteen years old and was traveling on my own throughout Australia.

Travel has been one of my biggest teachers of resilience. Throughout my adventures around the world, I have been in some sticky situations. I often envision my journeys to be just as self-empowering as Cheryl Strayed's in *Wild* or Elizabeth Gilbert's in *Eat, Pray, Love*. Yet, somehow, my adventures always seem to end up being awkward and probably somewhat imagined like Ben Stiller's in *The Secret Life of Walter Mitty*.

Still, I've gotten to do some pretty cool things:

- skydiving in California
- parasailing in Mexico
- bungee jumping in New Zealand
- holding koalas and feeding roos in Australia
- roasting marshmallows at the top of a volcano in Guatemala
- floating in the Dead Sea in Israel

Vacations are amazing. Necessary, too! Even Jesus took trips. And when He got away, then He would reconnect with His Father, who would refresh His spirit and renew His strength (see Luke 5:16).

When I became a legal adult, I believed that I needed to get away. I wanted to express my freedom and my newfound independence. So I decided to go to Australia. Just like that. I can't pinpoint what exactly attracted me to that country. Most of the things that I do simply spring up as planted passions in my heart, and, steadfastly, I pursue them with everything in me.

I used to believe that if only I could travel—if only I could get as far, far away as possible—then I would feel free. I read inspirational quotes on Pinterest like "traveling isn't always about running away from things, sometimes it's about running into what you truly want." The problem is that I did not know what it was that I wanted. I was prone to wander.

There are a lot of dreamers in this world. Dreamers, who come up with these extreme scenarios of grandeur ... but that is all that they do. They dream. Their imagination is as far as they go. Then there are people like me. Wanderers who follow every little idea that pops into our heads because we are adventurers! We aren't afraid to try new things! We are searching for our purpose! We have wanderlust! Sometimes, our travels bring us to cool destinations. Yet, when we return home with our hands full of treasures, we find that our hearts are empty.

A sedentary lifestyle is unhealthy, but so is an impulsive one. So how do we find the balance? We can come up with dreams and game plans for our careers, our families, our friendships, our vacations, our ministries, and even if these dreams come true, they will never fulfill our souls. Planted passions do not merely provide us with plenty to do or plenty to have; instead, they point us to God and petition that we pursue Him.

Listen carefully, those of you who *make your plans and* say, "We are traveling to this city in the next few days. We'll stay there for one year while our business explodes and revenue is up." The reality is you have no idea where your life will take you tomorrow. You are like a mist that appears one moment and then vanishes another. It would be best to say, "If it is the Lord's will and we live long enough, we hope to do this project or pursue that dream." But your current speech indicates an arrogance *that does not acknowledge the One who controls the universe,* and this kind of big talking is the epitome of evil. So if you know the right way to live and ignore it, it is sin—*plain and simple* (James 4:13–17 The Voice).

In Proverbs, it says that "a man's mind plans his way [as he journeys through life], but the Lord directs his steps and establishes them" (Proverbs 16:9 AMP). This is more than a physical plan or mulish mandate about where to take our next vacation or what our zip code should be. This is about directing our decisions toward God and surrendering the consequences to Him. When we expand our expectations, then He will provide us with plenty.

Sometimes, in the end, yes, that can mean expanding our tent stakes. The Bible is chock-full of scenarios where God told His people to physically go. "Get up and *go,*" God told Abraham. "Leave your country. Leave your relatives and your father's home, and travel to the land I will show you. Don't worry—I will guide you there" (see Genesis 12:1).

How scary would that be? God told Abraham to go, but notice that *He didn't say where.* That much uncertainty would terrify me! But Abraham didn't let it bother him. Instead, he listened; he didn't worry, and God guided him every step of the way. In fact, God never stopped. For generation after generation, He never stopped guiding and guarding Abraham's family. He carried out His promise through Ishmael and Isaac, then Jacob and Esau, through the twelve tribes, and beyond!

Jacob even planned a vacation in response to God's goodness. "We are now going to Bethel, where I will build an altar to the God who answered my prayers when I was in distress. He has been with me wherever I have gone" (Genesis 35:3 NLT). He never leaves us alone to fend for ourselves. He journeys with us.

So sometimes it is not good enough to just stay still. Jesus didn't!

> Jesus: No, I cannot stay. I need to preach the
> kingdom of God to other cities too. This is the
> purpose I was sent to fulfill (Luke 4:43 The Voice).

There was once a Christian named Ananias. God instructed him to go meet up with Saul, a notorious Christian-killer. "But Lord!" was Ananias's initial and justifiable response. "I've heard many people talk about the terrible things this man has done to the believers in Jerusalem! And he is authorized by the leading priests to arrest everyone who calls upon your name" (Acts 5:13a, 13b–14 NLT).

> The Lord: *Yes, but* you must go! I have chosen him
> to be My instrument to bring My name far and
> wide—to outsiders, to kings, and to the people of
> Israel as well (Acts 9:15 The Voice).

Ananias ended up playing a meaningful role in the metamorphosis from the sinful Saul to the apostolic Paul. "As time passed, Saul's confidence grew stronger and stronger, so much so that he debated with the Jews of Damascus and made an irrefutable case that Jesus is, in fact, God's Anointed, *the Liberating King*" (Acts 9:22 The Voice). After Damascus, Paul preached and launched churches in multiple countries across Europe and Asia. He wrote at least thirteen books of the Bible.

And Ananias's obedience played a big part in that. Sure, he began with a little bit of doubt. But if we really think about it, we insert doubts into our own faith a lot, too.

"But God, it's scary."

"But God, I'm not qualified."

"But God, I don't want to do it alone."

I'm sure when God hears these pleas that He laughs. "Oh, child. Haven't you figured it out by now?"

The situation may be scary.

But God.

God is bigger.

You may not have the qualifications.

But God.

God specializes in turning shepherds into kings.

You may feel all alone.

But God.

God is with you and will never leave you.

Paul's passion led him to prison—multiple times. Is your pursuit to spread the love of God passionate enough, strong enough, worthy enough to take you to prison? It sounds scary, but this is kind of the life that we signed up for. It sounds scary, but God. Our God is a chain-breaking, wall-crumbling kind of God. Amen?

Now, understand that we also have to obey when God says no to going far or leaving for now. My pastor, Brenden Brown, always says that "not everyone is called to cross oceans, but everyone can cross their street." God doesn't just provide us with planted passions, He plants us exactly where we are to pursue those around us. You may have heard of the Great Commission. After Jesus died, He conquered death and came to life (hallelujah!), and as Jesus was ascending into heaven, He left His disciples with this instruction:

> *Here's the knowledge you need:* you will receive power when the Holy Spirit comes on you. And you will be My witnesses, first here in Jerusalem, then beyond to Judea and Samaria, and finally to the farthest places on earth. (Acts 1:8 The Voice)

First, here.

Then, beyond.

Finally, farther.

You have to start where you are. It seems funny, because when

He called the disciples into ministry originally, Jesus said that they had to leave everything behind to follow Him wherever He went. When He encountered certain people along the way, Jesus would command them to follow as well. In some cases, however, that was not the case:

> When they get to the other side of the lake, in the Gerasene country opposite Galilee, a man from the city is waiting for Jesus when He steps out of the boat. The man is full of demonic spirits. He's been running around for a long time stark naked, and he's homeless, sleeping among the dead in a cemetery. This man has on many occasions been tied up and chained and kept under guard, but each time he has broken free and the demonic power has driven him back into remote places away from human contact. Jesus commands the demonic force to leave him. The man looks at Jesus and starts screaming. He falls down in front of Jesus.
>
> Possessed Man *(shouting)*: Don't torment me, Jesus, Son of the Most High God! Why are You here?
>
> Jesus *(calmly and simply)*: What's your name?
>
> Possessed Man: Battalion.
>
> He says this because an army of demons is inside of him. The demons start begging Jesus not to send them into the bottomless pit. They plead instead to enter into a herd of pigs feeding on a steep hillside near the shore. Jesus gives them permission to do so. Suddenly the man is liberated from the demons, but the pigs—they stampede, squealing down the hill and into the lake where they drown themselves.

The pig owners see all this. They run back to their town and tell everyone in the region about it. Soon a crowd rushes from the town to see what's going on out by the lake. There they find Jesus seated *to teach* with the newly liberated man sitting at His feet *learning in the posture of a disciple*. This former madman is now properly dressed and completely sane. This frightens the people. The pig owners tell them the whole story—the healing, *the pigs' mass suicide, everything*.

The people are scared to death, and they don't want this scary abnormality happening in their territory. They ask Jesus to leave immediately. *Jesus doesn't argue.* He prepares to leave, but before they embark, the newly liberated man begs to come along and join the band of disciples.

Jesus: No. Go home. Tell your people this amazing story about how much God has done for you.

The man does so. In fact, he tells everyone in the whole city how much Jesus did for him that day *on the shore*. (Luke 8:26–39 The Voice)

First, here.

Then, beyond.

Finally, farther.

Placement is paramount to God's planning. Jesus knew that the previously possessed man's story would make the biggest impact in his own town where the people knew about his past. They were used to averting their eyes when he would have an episode. Perhaps they had to assist with placing the chains around his wrists and body when the fits became bad. But God. God turned him into a clad, lucid, respectable man.

Timing is also part of the orchestration for God's operation.

When He told Abraham to get up and go, the land was not ready for him to inhibit yet. It actually belonged to the Canaanites at the time. So Abraham had to move on and live in Egypt for a while. Sometimes, God says, "Not yet."

First, here.

Then, beyond.

Finally, farther.

When Jesus says to go home, and God says not yet, it is not time to be discouraged. There is much to do wherever you are! Christopher J. H. Wright says that, "the mission of God's people is far too big to be left only to missionaries." There is need everywhere, even in your hometown.

Mother Teresa believed the same thing. "Stay where you are. Find your own Calcutta. Find the sick, the suffering, and the lonely right where you are—in your own homes and in your own families, in your workplaces and in your schools ... You can find Calcutta all over the world, if you have the eyes to see. Everywhere, wherever you go, you find people who are unwanted, unloved, uncared for, just rejected by society—completely forgotten, completely left alone." It's what the disciples did:

> Peter and John went to the Temple one afternoon to take part in the three o'clock prayer service. As they approached the Temple, a man lame from birth was being carried in. Each day he was put beside the Temple gate, the one called the Beautiful Gate, so he could beg from the people going into the Temple. When he saw Peter and John about to enter, he asked them for some money.
>
> Peter and John looked at him intently, and Peter said, "Look at us!" The lame man looked at them eagerly, expecting some money. But Peter said, "I don't have any silver or gold for you. But

I'll give you what I have. In the name of Jesus Christ the Nazarene, get up and walk!"

Then Peter took the lame man by the right hand and helped him up. And as he did, the man's feet and ankles were instantly healed and strengthened. He jumped up, stood on his feet, and began to walk! Then, walking, leaping, and praising God, he went into the Temple with them. (Acts 3:1–8 NLT)

Peter and John were just taking their typical trip to the temple. Then an opportunity arose for them to share the grace of God, and they seized it. It's easy to walk past beggars in the street, and we may not be blessed with the gift of healing like Peter. But God. God makes all things possible. What I love about this story is that Peter commanded the man to get up and walk, but he then went over and personally helped him up. Peter did everything that he could. But God. God did the healing.

That is our role, friend, our role as Christians, our role as a church. We are to lift one another up, encourage one another, and direct the attention to the power of God. As a Christian, it is my mission to know God and to make Him known. A few years back, I scribbled this prayer on the inside cover of my Bible:

Wherever.

Whenever.

Whatever.

It is not my job to predict or to know the reply to my prayer. God will guide my steps and will communicate my calling in His perfect timing. Until then, I can just be the girl who went where she knew there were needs and found ways to meet them.

Jessica Sage

Verse for Thought

> "He was saying to them, 'The harvest is abundant [for there are many who need to hear the good news about salvation], but the workers [those available to proclaim the message of salvation] are few. Therefore, [prayerfully] ask the Lord of the harvest to send out workers into His harvest.'" (Luke 10:2 AMP)

Reflection Question

Where is your Calcutta?

Let Us Pray

Oh God,
I lift up in prayer those who are working on Your harvest.
Keep them safe and give them what they need.
Lord, break my heart for what breaks Yours.
Send me where and when You need me;
Until then, use me where I am now,
For I am Yours,
and You are mine.
Amen.

18

Thoughts of a Missionary

I am not a "real" missionary. Not yet, at least. And by "real" I mean a full-time, sponsored missionary who lives in a dangerous part of the world, who risks her life every day by courageously fighting off all evil and poverty and hunger and terrorism, all the while barefoot and spinning around in a maxi skirt. I'm talking Amy Carmichael, Katie Davis, and Mother Theresa all wrapped into one.

One day, I hope to be her. For now, I take little trips. In the past six months, I have been on two mission trips to Guatemala. Stripping away the comfort of familiarity and leaving home to join up with other planet-shaking strangers was not easy. There were many bumps in the road, but the journey was life changing.

In the beginning, Guatemala wasn't even in my travel plans. It had all started with some shoes—a pair of boots, actually. My heart was set on finding the exact light blueish, gray booties that were so clearly pictured in my head. My mom and I spent hours scouring the mall for the perfect pair. We stopped at every shoe store, and I tried on hundreds of boots. Each pair was too something. Too suede. Too tall. Too blue. Too gray.

Head low and shoulders slumped, I agreed to go into one last store before heading home. There they were. My perfect pair of not-too-blue-not-too-gray boots with no heel. It must have been my lucky day because they were on sale *and* the cashier gave me a coupon.

Thrilled, I took my boots home and proudly displayed them in my closet—where they stayed on display for weeks. Every time I wanted to wear them, I could not shake a guilty feeling in my gut. I had no idea what was spurring this feeling. When I could no longer withstand the guilt, I drove back to the store and returned the boots.

That night, I attended the evening service at my church. An emergency response video was played to raise funds to support Haiti's recent earthquake. My heart started racing. That was it. That was the reason why I felt guilty buying my boots. I was supposed to invest my money elsewhere. I raced down the aisle and dropped my cash that I had received from returning my boots into the offering basket. As soon as I did, a whisper pulsed throughout my innermost being, "*Go, my daughter.*" Immediately, I knew. I needed to go to Haiti. I sped home and immediately began looking up mission trips to the hurting country.

This was not the first time that I had researched Haiti. I was a freshman in high school when a big earthquake shook the small nation in 2010. A few friends and I rallied together to organize bake sales and administer car washes to raise money for the cause. We named our group *Lespwa*, which means "hope" in Haitian Creole.

I ended up applying to go to Haiti over New Year's through the organization Adventures in Missions and was immediately accepted. A few weeks later, however, I received an email stating that unfortunately the trip was overbooked, and alternatively they had an opening for me to join the team going to Antigua, Guatemala. I expected anger and disappointment to seize me, but instead a wave of peace flowed through me. "Well," I started telling people, "I guess God wants me in Guatemala instead!"

As I agreed to transfer over my application, I was comforted and confident as I remembered Solomon's wise words, "In their hearts humans plan their course, but the Lord establishes their steps" (Proverbs 16:9 NIV). This was another step in my journey here on earth. I was so excited to leave my home for a short time so that those I reached could have a home in heaven for eternity. However, I hit it off with a rocky start:

28 December 2016

As I write, I can glimpse out of my peripheral the glimmer from the alligator tears still rolling down my cheeks. At least now they are just cute alligator tears (or I hope they are cute) instead of the big ole ugly cry tears that were streaming down my face only a few minutes ago. The two waterfall stains on my face and the bubbly snot streak on my sleeve have earned me many disapproving and disgusted looks.

Why am I so miserable, you ask? Right now, I am logging my story at a Samsung phone charging station in the Mexico City airport when I should be arriving in Guatemala to rendezvous with the rest of my mission team. But mostly I am upset because I am writing with an airport gift shop Mexican matador pen instead of my favorite Sharpie pen that I forgot at home. Just kidding (sort of).

This is your typical case of delayed and rescheduled flights, and I normally wouldn't mind spending a few extra hours in an airport. We twentysomething solo international travelers refer to trips like these as the Backpackers Marathon, where we purposefully book multiple layover flights just to save a few bucks.

In the case of this trip, however, I am not completely a solo traveler. I am flying alone, yes, but only to meet up with a team through Adventures in Missions to serve in Guatemala for a week. We are scheduled to build a house, hold a soup kitchen, visit hospitals, orphanages, etc. Our scheduled meeting time is 1:00 p.m.—which is ten minutes from now; yet, here I am in Mexico with an almost dead phone and flimsy free Wi-Fi that literally only works in this one row of chairs.

I have not met any of the members of my team yet, nor the team leader. I have email addresses for both my American and Guatemalan correspondents, so I have sent them both messages notifying them of my predicament. However, I have not heard back from either, and needless to say I am majorly stressed, hence all the tears.

It is important to note that I happen to find myself in situations like this quite frequently in my adventures. It has come to my attention that many of my features and characteristics resemble those of the many unfortunate, young, female Americans that get kidnapped and sent to other countries for prostitution and terrorism activity. Thus, I am always targeted in airports, but I praise God for His continual protection, and ultimately, I don't mind the extra security precautions that come my way.

In this trip alone, I was flagged in my initial TSA screening because of the small metal zippers in my Adidas sweatpants pockets. I was promptly pulled aside and given not one but two additional pat downs. Then, on my first layover, I failed the initial customs screening coming into Mexico. I was ushered to a table where an officer opened and unpacked all my bags. This literally happens to me every time; so much so that my family penned the slogan "Only you, Jess." I have been covered in bomb powder too many times to count; even the last time I went to Disneyland, I was pulled aside for a second security screening upon entry. It's so sad that it's funny.

But it is in these moments that it is pivotal to remember that God is in control. He has a perfect plan, and I am living it out right now. How is He using my ugly cry for good? I am not sure at the moment ... but maybe He will tell me later.

This past Christmas season has taught me a lot about the importance of Jesus's presence as the Prince of Peace in my life. Being college age in a rapidly advancing world presents a lot of pressure for goals + fulfillment, titles + reimbursements, money + success. But then it also encourages an adventurous and wandering lifestyle where you should just chase after whatever it is you feel like.

But how are you supposed to know which is the right thing to do? I have been chasing after both—I have been pursuing two separate careers to find my *position in this world* and am pursuing travel (hence this trip) to find my *place in this world*. But let me tell you, it is not healthy. I find myself exhausted, stressed, and drowning in my ugly cry tears.

Perhaps what God is trying to teach me is that my *purpose in this world* is not to focus on the *title* or the *travel*, but to rely on His *truth*: we are His vessels, broken + beautiful, here to seek out + love His precious lost children.

Looking back, I know that God was trying to capture and cleanse my heart before I started my adventure. Once I found Wi-Fi, I connected with my mom, who calmed me down, and my best friend, who pointed out that God must really want me in Guatemala if the devil was trying that hard to stop me. My favorite Bible verse rang through my head: "We knew our enemies' intent was to intimidate us into stopping our work. They reasoned, 'These Jews will stop rebuilding out of fear and discouragement. Progress will grind to a halt.' Instead I renewed my dedication, strengthened my hands" (Nehemiah 6:9 The Voice). God assured me that it was all about *His* timing and *His* purpose, not mine.

I met my team the next day. We were led by our American correspondent, Gary, as well as a local Guatemalan pastor, Luis. My worrisome heart had formed presuppositions that everyone else would already be seasoned missionaries, much older and wiser than me, be so fluent in Spanish that they would be welcomed by the Guatemalans as natives, and leaving me behind as a foolish, young outsider not understanding their beautiful tongues. It's amazing how far you can get when you allow worry to consume you.

Instead, God had assembled a dream team of incredible individuals from all over the United States. No one knew much Spanish, but we had two group leaders to translate for us, and honestly, I think the Guatemalans received us better because we were *not* good, but we were trying. We all worked together well, could communicate with one another clearly, and formed lasting friendships.

Before the trip, we were given ideas on what to bring as donations to give out throughout the week. Our itinerary was full of different activities, most of which involved playing with kids, so we brought a lot of toys and toiletries to bring along each day, including the first one:

29 December 2017

The first thing that we did today was visit a cross that overlooked Antigua to reflect on why we are here. The city is rich in history, with its many churches and cobblestone roads, but is heavily influenced by the West and modern technology. Beginning with this reflection time was a great start to the week.

Afterward, we went to the orphanage wing of a cerebral palsy hospital and spent some time getting to know the children's stories. Some had more severe cases than others, but they all had such a sparkle in their eyes. We were given the opportunity to bottle-feed the kids, and the girl that I was feeding wasn't able to suck out of the bottle, so I had to slowly pour the drink into her mouth bit by bit. It was incredible to see and understand that God made us all different—none of us fit into this world's definition of "normal." We are all created differently so that altogether we can come together as God's beautiful masterpiece.

This evening we worked together and cooked a soup out of broth and vegetables. We packed it up and hopped in our chicken bus to meet up with some members of Pastor Luis's church to find homeless to feed. It took some searching, but we fed around fifteen people and were able to pray for several of them.

30 December 2017

Day two was construction day. We started out
with the upstairs level of a home designed to house
widows and their children. I spent the majority
of the time painting a portion of the floor; first
we covered it with an acid wash and then after it
dried, we applied a coat of acrylic combined with
paint thinner.

We went to our second construction site. This
one was located in a more impoverished area on
a mountainside. Part of the neighbor's backyard
had begun to landslide into the construction, so
Raphael—a member of Pastor Luis's church and
our strong construction instructor—had filled
one-hundred-pound flour bags with dirt. Our
job was to carry them over and strategically place
them in order to create a firm wall to prevent more
of the neighbor's backyard from collapsing. It took
a lot of team work and hefty effort, but we did it!

31 December 2017

On New Year's Eve day, we began with prayer. We
had come up with a list of specific prayer requests
for the church and the city and then once again
piled into the chicken bus with members of Pastor
Luis's church. Initially, we were worried because
some of us didn't speak Spanish, but Pastor Luis
assured us that although we speak two different
languages, God still hears us.

So as we drove around the city border, we
began praying for each request, one by one,

alternating between the members of the church in Spanish and the members of our mission team in English. Oh, how beautiful it was to talk to God with different languages but one voice; it gave us just a small glimpse into the future when every knee will bow and worship our Father altogether.

Our next event was our VBS that we brainstormed and created as a team. (VBS, vacation Bible school, usually contains a story, music, games, crafts, and snacks and is designed to point toward the incredible, life-changing story of Jesus Christ.) The chicken bus dropped us off in the middle of a neighborhood where a family from the church lived. While planning, we had no idea how many kids were coming, or how old they would be, so we were a little anxious. But soon droves of children flocked in.

We began with some songs, and then I delivered a short salvation story that God had given me the night before. When I asked afterward if any of the kids wanted to pray with me and accept Jesus Christ as their Savior, over forty kids raised their hands! That was when I knew that this is what I want to do with the rest of my life.

We then split the kids into two groups and sent half to do crafts and half to play games. Overall, it was a success, and we had a blast!

After lunch, we took a much bigger, public chicken bus to the market for sightseeing and shopping.

Equipped with our house's address, we were instructed to find our own transportation home via tuk-tuk. We were so excited to finally be able to take one! So three of us piled into one, and the driver started off on what was supposed to be a fifteen-minute journey. After a while, we noticed the driver turn around … and then turn around again … and then turn around again. We laughed as we asked the driver about the address.

We did not speak Spanish, and he did not speak English, but we were able to gather that we were house number seventeen, and the neighborhood he took us to did not have a house number seventeen, probably because that was not our neighborhood! Our driver was definitely lost. After asking three different pedestrians and the police, no one could help us. By now, we were freaking out, and I ended up calling our American correspondent from earlier to get ahold of Pastor Luis to get ahold of our American guide to get ahold of our driver. Over an hour later, we made it home for our New Year's Eve service!

It was an amazing way to end 2016.

1 January 2017

One of the girls in our group had done this same trip the year before and had fallen in love with one of the kids at an orphanage that they had visited. Our plan for the day was to go to a different orphanage for an appointment from –11:00 a.m. to 1:00 p.m. and then swing by her orphanage on the way home. Pastor Luis was with his family for the day, so we piled into a van.

After a really long drive, we noticed our driver turn around … again … and again. It was like déjà vu. But almost a full round of "One Hundred

Bottles of Coke on the Wall" later, we made it to the orphanage. By this time, our appointment was almost over, but it did not matter because they had actually taken all of the kids to the beach. Discouraged, we decided to just head over to the second orphanage.

Once we arrived, we had an incredible time playing with the kids! We brought bubbles, toys, games, balls, and just loved on all the children for hours. I was reminded of Jesus's *precious promise,* "*I will not leave you as orphans, I will come to you*" (John 14:18 The Voice).

2 January 2017

Since today is our last day, we had free time and braved a hike up the active Volcán de Pacaya. Some hiked, some rode horses. It was hands down the most difficult hike I have ever done, but once we arrived at the top, it was totally worth it!

Our guide, who was eighty-one years old, brought us skewers and amazing flavored marshmallows to roast! It was such a surreal experience.

Located at the top of the volcano is a little tienda hut. The workers inside told us that it was recognized by *National Geographic* as the most uniquely located store in the world because each time the volcano erupts, they have to relocate (obviously). They also instructed us that they were on code orange for the day, which meant that the volcano could go off at any minute! He showed us pictures of the last eruption and half-jokingly said, "Be ready to run!"

On the way home, most of us were sleeping, but one person was able to catch a picture of the volcano erupting! What!

12 January 2017

The last twenty-four hours of the journey were rough for me, as I was suffering from food poisoning. I warned my family that when they picked me up, I would be disgusting and covered in tears, snot, and vomit. When they realized that the tears, snot, and vomit were mine and not from serving, it made the whole situation funnier.

Even though the sickness wasn't fun, I wouldn't change anything about the trip. I did not want to leave, and as the plane took off, I could feel a big piece of my heart being torn out and left behind.

Since being back in America, it has been a difficult adjustment having experienced the reality of God in a part of the world that does not recognize Him as King. I long every day to go back to that orphanage and to rejoin my teammates in furthering God's kingdom again. For now, I have been praying that the fiery passion would be rekindled here in America, in my hometown, and in my workplace.

I recently completed reading through the book of John, and the last chapter really stood out to me. It takes place after Jesus's death and resurrection. The disciples have already encountered Jesus a few times in His risen body, and in this encounter, they are out fishing but with no luck. Jesus appears and instructs them to throw their nets out on the other side. Suddenly their nets fill with fish.

This incident is Jesus's way of showing the disciples that their old ways of living will leave them as empty as their nets; their old habits will do nothing for them. But now that they have experienced Jesus, their lives have been impacted and changed forever. They can't go back now.

Here's to never looking back.

My love for the country only strengthened the longer that I was away. It was just three short months before Guatemala and I were reunited again. This time, I spent the entire duration of the trip at the orphanage that we had visited back on New Year's Day. The orphanage has a small one-room apartment in the backyard for volunteers and child sponsors to come and visit, so I arranged to stay there in exchange for help with a painting project.

10 March 2017
9:50 a.m., Panama City, Panama

"Prepare for takeoff." The emergency video is playing on the screens fixed on the backs of the plane seats. Spanish instructions spew out of the speakers. It has occurred to me that I have not yet met my one goal that I set the last time I was in Latin America: to learn Spanish.

This trip is going smoothly so far. This is a dangerous thought to declare, considering my track record and the fact that the last time I boarded a plane, it did not take off.

My assigned seat is 30D: on the aisle. That does not really matter though, because I am the only one in this whole row. I set my passport on the middle seat to keep me company and welcome the sunlight that crept its way in through the half-opened window shade. Now it's a party.

It is my typical routine to haggle my brother out of his window seat so that I can watch the world pass me by at a hundred thousand miles per hour. Like the loyal brother that he is, he always lets me have it. He is smarter than I'll ever be; he has discovered the inevitable truth: that a happy Jess equals a happy life.

Besides the obvious perks of the view and Instagram shots, window seats are also good for the side headrest. This is for those occasions when you are tired of your lower neck stiffening like a giraffe as you sleep. Instead, you can channel your inner pigeon and permanently stiffen your neck at an obscene angle. It's very attractive.

I stay in my aisle seat though, keeping my option of stretching my legs in the center aisle open. Also, the aisle seat provides me with a beeline to the bathroom because I'm a lightweight when it comes to peeing. I know it is useless though because the chances of my body allowing me to pee in a plane bathroom is the same as using a port-a-potty, swimming in the ocean, or while camping in the woods: zero. I am comforted by the availability of my options, however.

There isn't anything great about the middle seat. The unwritten rule states that the person sitting in the middle seat is the proud owner of the armrests, but that never actually happens. I suppose that if you are a social person, then it can be great because you have not one but two new prospective friends to talk to. I thought that I was not that said social person, but today I have proved that is not the case.

On my first flight, I sat next to a larger Panama native who spoke only Spanish and in rapidly strung shouts to his companion across the aisle. Due to my lack of Spanish vernacular, we did not converse beyond a friendly greeting.

Then my gruff, slurring window-seat pal arrived. He, too, was a San Francisco Bay Area native, only he actually lived in the city, in the Tenderloin district. He was visiting Panama for the umpteenth time; this was his first time vacationing without his girlfriend before they move there.

Upon telling him that Panama was just my pit stop to Guatemala, where I was going to serve at an orphanage for the week, his eyes lit up. He began to tell me that when he was in his twenties, he was a devout follower of Mother Theresa. Inspired by her teachings, he packed up his belongings and flew to Calcutta, where he fed the hungry and bandaged the injured.

"I'd never been into ... you know ... good stuff like that. But there was something about being there with other people just doing good things that felt right, like we were connected." I smiled because I knew exactly what he meant. The lights dimmed, and we slept, him a pigeon and I a giraffe. Meanwhile my Panama friend shouted to his friend about the Spanish sitcom streaming on their TV screens.

11 March 2017
7:06 a.m., San Lucas, Guatemala

My prayer for the day:
God, I trust You.
Fill me with a radiant peace.
Use me.

7:01 p.m.

My day was mostly filled with playing with the kids. If I were able to, I would adopt one of the little boys named Gerson. He has a prosthetic leg, but that doesn't stop him from following his dream of becoming a professional soccer player. All the kids are adorable, but Gerson is always the first to smile and wave. He loves Curious George and has a giant book containing a collection of stories. Each page contains a paragraph in Spanish and then a paragraph with the English translation. Today he asked me to read every story twice through. As I watch him play with the other kids, I can see why he likes the book so much. He is just like the little monkey.

My curious Gerson.

14 March 2017
6:48 p.m.

I met an American group that came to visit the orphanage today. They thought that I spoke Spanish, so they invited me over to help. When the leader realized that they still needed translation, he took over. I stayed off to the side to learn more about the orphanage. It has been hard to engage with the language barrier, so I figured that this was my chance. What touched me the most was that the American leader who was translating advised the group that if any of them wished to volunteer in the future, then they needed to assess their skills. "Anyone can hold a baby. That doesn't help anyone."

Ouch.

Why am I here then?

From now on, I am here to help. Laundry? Dishes? Cooking? You name it.

15 March 2017
1:50 p.m.

I can tell that the kids are well taken care of all year long and on a regular basis. They are definitely raised right. They use their manners and know about Jesus.

Although it is sad that they are not raised by their own parents, they have loving tias and are always surrounded by friends. They are provided with ample clothing of trending brands decorated with pop culture characters like Mickey Mouse and Iron Man and Angry Birds. To my surprise, they have a TV and cable to educate them about all these popular icons.

Initially, I was jealous that they have all these nice things that I never had as a kid: nice clothes, TV, a trampoline ... but now I am grateful for them that they are this blessed.

As tiny humans, they naturally quarrel, but they knock it off when they are told and immediately obey when they are told to help out with chores. They are the most obedient kids that I have ever met. I will miss them.

I have not been using Wi-Fi this entire time. It has been incredibly refreshing to detox. But I am worried that an emergency has occurred at home because I have not told my family the name of the orphanage or a way to contact me. Last night, I had a terrible nightmare that something happened to my mom and that she needed emergency surgery. I woke up to what I thought was the sound of my brother's voice. I'm sure everything is fine, but I miss them so much.

18 March 2017
10:04 p.m., Somewhere over the Mexican/US Border

Only an hour and a half until I am home! It has been a long day, and this flight could not feel any longer. There was some pretty rough turbulence, and I was admittedly frightened. I preoccupied myself by watching *La La Land* and *Me Before You*. Both films have heartbreaking endings, where the characters fulfill their dreams but their dreams don't turn out how they had anticipated.

It is so hard not knowing how things will turn out, or if they even will turn out. Tears stream down my face as I ask myself, *Why am I here? What am I good at?* I aspire to do big things with my life. They say that the world is changed by the people who believe they can.

My friend asked me earlier what my pet peeves are. I decided that they are when people make fun of my voice and when I receive comments on my

age. I'm tired of being told that I'm still young.
That I still have time.

But what about now? I'm rushing back to my real life at five
hundred miles per hour and am unsure about what I am going
to do once I land. At church we sing a song with lyrics that are
currently pouring out of my innermost being:

> Set a fire down in my soul,
> That I can't contain,
> That I can't control ...
>
> Equipped with my passion and my story, Lord, I'm
> here and I'm ready.
> Use me.
> May my life echo Your truth day in and day out.

Verse for Thought

> "One day, the Eternal One called out to Abram.
> Eternal One: *Abram,* get up and go! Leave your country. Leave your relatives and your father's home, and travel to the land I will show you. *Don't worry—I will guide you there.*" (Genesis 12:1 The Voice)

Reflection Question

Is God calling you to go?

Let Us Pray

> *Here I am, Lord.*
> *Take me as I am.*
> *Consume me, transform me.*
> *Break my heart for what breaks Yours.*
> *I ask that You illuminate the right path for me.*
> *Wherever You call me to go, I will go.*
> *Whenever You call me to go, I will go.*
> *Whatever You call me to do, I will do.*
> *Amen.*

19

A Tribute to Earth, Wind, and Fire

No, not the band. But the actual earth, wind, and fire.

It is a blistering 108 degrees outside, but as I write, I am wrapped up nice and cozy in my pajamas. I gaze down at the mystery stain located on the bridge of my white t-shirt that stretches across my chest. *Did I accidentally vomit on myself?* I just came home from spending exactly thirteen minutes at work before realizing that I was too queasy to last an hour let alone the rest of my shift. *Is it dog goo?* My older-than-ancient doggo has been balding and oozing unidentifiable substances for a while now. The stain is too light to be coffee or the chocolate muffin from breakfast but is too dark to be the remnants of tears from my sobfest earlier.

This has been quite the year for tears.

This has been quite the year, *period.*

Right now, my blood brother is also at home sick and asleep in the room adjacent to mine. My stepbrother is at his school wearing the same outfit as yesterday and was instructed to skip picture day to wait for the makeup day, when he can wear a proper outfit and get his hair cut. My mom is stressed, worried, but reluctantly at work because she was threatened with getting fired if she missed another day. Meanwhile, my step-dad is in the ICU, alone and close to death.

The same stepdad whom we welcomed into our family only three months ago is now fighting for his life. What first started out as the flu turned into strep, then toxic shock syndrome, and then kidney failure.

Why? Why is this happening, God?

But my cry is less in anguish and more of curiosity. By now, I am sure you have noticed that weird things happen to me and my family quite often. Instead of labeling my life as an enigma and dwelling in the bewilderment, I trust in the Lord.

He shifts my "Why is this happening?" into "What can I learn from this?"

Many times in the Bible, during church services, in books, on podcasts, and in songs, artists and speakers like to implement analogies that liken God and faith to nature references. Examples include:

> Water: waves, ocean, flood, river
> Fire: flames, blaze, refiner's fire
> Trees: mustard seeds, olive trees, date palm trees,
> vine

Each of the elements are significant. Water refreshes. Air revives. Fire refines. Earth retains. The earth is one beautiful, magnanimous creation conceived to glorify God and to serve as our temporary home! It is no wonder why they reflect so much of who God is and what we encounter every day through nature. I don't know about you, but I am so, so grateful that God spent the time to uniquely handcraft each detail: all the animals, every leaf, each sea. As we navigate through the seasons—seasons of sun or satisfaction, rain or ruin, wind or worry, fire or fury—we can rest assured knowing that *we are never alone.* That is what water always reminds me.

Living along the coast, I like to visit the beach and observe the ocean. Looking out at the long, flat horizon makes me feel so small and powerless yet at the same time so loved and in awe. How could a God who is as vast as the sky love me as deep as the sea? I have heard it said that you shouldn't cross oceans for people who wouldn't cross a puddle for you. But I serve a God who *made* the oceans for me. He loves me and has called me to love others with that same unconditional love. Taking the time to love on people may change their lives forever. And if it doesn't—if they beat me down and break me in retaliation—then God will show up and build me back stronger with resilience.

We know that storms come. Jesus and His disciples were besieged with many storms, both emotional and physical. Did you catch that? Jesus was besieged by storms. *Jesus.* Yet, He did not let them stir Him; He did not sit and stew over them. Instead, He spent the time in the storm strengthening His children's faith. I love how Max Lucado puts it: "Getting on board with Christ can mean getting soaked with Christ." Following Jesus doesn't exclude us from experiencing storms, sorrow, or suffering. Instead, following Jesus gives us the assurance of safety. He is the ultimate lifeguard: one who defies and disregards the potential and power of water and can walk right over it!

But He still calls us out upon the water, like He did with Peter. He does it like how a father may teach his child how to swim or how to swing on the monkey bars: He lets go and leaves some space for growth and independence but not so much as to compromise security. And He always assures His child that He is right there.

> Jesus: Be still. It is I. You have nothing to fear.
> (Matthew 14:27 The Voice)

The key to remember is that it is *with* God that we can walk on water. It is *with* God that all things are possible. It is "*with* God's power working in us, [that] God can do much, much more than anything we can ask or imagine" (Ephesians 3:20 NCV). The moment that we assume that we can carry on in our own power, the moment that our eyes stray from Jesus, we begin to sink like Peter did:

> Peter stepped out of the boat onto the water and began walking toward Jesus. But when he remembered how strong the wind was, his courage caught in his throat and he began to sink.
> Peter: Master, save me!
> Immediately Jesus reached for Peter and caught him.
> Jesus: O you of little faith. Why did you doubt *and dance back and forth between following* Me *and heeding fear?* (Matthew 14:29b–31 The Voice)

Time and again, Jesus demonstrates that we are not responsible for the doing but for the believing. In the test, we must trust, and He will do the rest. That is exactly what happened with Shadrach, Meshach, and Abednego. Often, the Bible refers to trials as a refiner's fire. Like a refiner who engulfs precious metals in fire to purify them, God allows us to be absorbed in adversity so that we may emerge free and spotless. "*Suffering tests* your faith which is more valuable than gold (remember that gold, although it is perishable, is tested by fire) so that if it is found genuine, you can receive praise, honor, and glory when Jesus the Anointed, *our Liberating King,* is revealed at last" (1 Peter 1:7 The Voice).

Shadrach, Meshach, and Abednego experienced a quite literal refiner's fire. Many years ago, King Nebuchadnezzar of Babylon deported the most handsome, physically fit, highly educated, powerful men from each land that he had conquered and placed them as interns to become part of his royal court (see Daniel 1:4). This move increased the king's government, crippled his conquered enemies, and ensured that his enemies would not attack the land their loved ones now inhabited. These new young, interns included Daniel, Shadrach, Meshach, and Abednego.

One day, King Nebuchadnezzar placed orders for a giant idol to be crafted out of gold, and then he declared that all his subjects bow down to worship it. But our valiant interns refused. Once the king heard about their insubordination, he ordered the consequences to be administered—they be thrown into a furnace of blazing fire. Through it all, our interns were not stirred.

> Shadrach, Meshach, and Abednego: Nebuchadnezzar, we have no need to defend our actions in this matter. *We are ready for the test.* If you throw us into the blazing furnace, then the God we serve is able to rescue us from a furnace of blazing fire and release us from your power, Your Majesty. But even if He does not, O king, you can be sure that we *still* will not serve your gods and we will not worship the golden statue you erected. (Daniel 3:16–18 The Voice)

Shadrach, Meshach, and Abednego were not worried. They did not react with performance, but with faith. And God showed up. He did not extinguish the fire; instead, He entered in *with* them and brought them out unsinged.

Their faith had a firm foundation, like a tree. Trees are often used in God's Word as analogies for how we live our lives and respond to the gift of our Father's grace. David wrote that "those who are devoted to God will flourish like *budding* date-palm trees; they will grow *strong and tall* like cedars in Lebanon. Those planted in the house of the Eternal will thrive in the courts of our God" (Psalm 92:12–13 The Voice).

Trees change with the seasons, just as we should. Yet trees do not worry, because God always provides for them through the change. In Jeremiah, God says blessed are the men who trust God through it all, the women who stick with God no matter what. They remain plugged in to an impenetrable source.

> They are like trees planted along a riverbank,
> with roots that reach deep into the water.
> Such trees are not bothered by the heat or worried
> by long months of drought.
> Their leaves stay green,
> and they never stop producing fruit. (Jeremiah
> 17:8 NLT)

Some trees actually *need* the heat, the same heat that can hurt, that can destroy. Olive trees, for example, need both heat and the cool to survive, says Lysa Terkeurst:

> First, in order to be fruitful, the olive tree has to have both the east wind and the west wind. The east wind is the dry, hot wind form the desert. This is a hard wind. So harsh that it can blow over green grass and make it completely wither in one day. The west wind, on the other hand, comes from the mediterranean. It brings rain and life. The olive tree needs both of these winds to produce fruit ... and so do we. We need both the winds of hardship and the winds of relief to sweep across our lives if we are to be truly fruitful.

If you find yourself in a deep, dark place; if you feel lost and alone and ashamed that you've buried yourself into a pit of shame, have faith. Have faith that God can transform your desperation from being buried into a position of being planted. Every seed has to grow through soil before it can soar into the sky. Once sprouted, saplings will encounter storms, but storms encourage deeper roots. Let the storms of life, the trials, the difficulties, encourage you to deepen your own roots. "Life rooted in God stands firm (Proverbs 12:3b MSG). Soak up the necessary nutrients through passionate worship, purposeful prayer, and persistent Bible reading.

And you have to believe it.

There was once a time when the disciples became frustrated because they were unable to heal a boy who suffered from epilepsy. The child's seizures would often cause him to fall into fires and rivers. Jesus drove out a demon that had taken up residency in the boy. In bewilderment, the disciples asked Jesus why they were unable to do it themselves. "Jesus answered, 'Because your faith is too small. I tell you the truth, if your faith is as big as a mustard seed, you can say to this mountain, 'Move from here to there,' and it will move. All things will be possible for you'" (Matthew 17:20 NCV).

It is easy to read the Bible and think, *My, what lovely parables.* But the Bible is not just a book of parables! It is a history book—*your* history book—of what was, what is, and what is to come. The power behind the transformative authority of the Bible comes from belief in the truth of its words and meanings. It makes me laugh when people say that they don't read the Bible because it is too boring or too hard to understand. Really? Have you *read* the Bible? It is an instruction manual for finances, sex, parenting, construction, leadership, you name it. If you are struggling, find a new translation. Sometimes all it takes is a change in method—not the message, mind you—and it will click!

You will feel refreshed.

You will be inspired.

You will understand why we go through what we go through.

When you pray "Your will be done," and sing "call me out upon the waters," God answers with "yes" and "amen."

And the fire burns.

The winds roar.

The waves crash.

And just as your firm, clenching grasp ahold, His steady, helping hand slowly slips away until it's just two fingers barely touching, and He whispers, "Be still."

And immediately, the fire evaporates.

The wind hides.

The water flattens.

Shaky, you emerge with the realization that you are stronger than before.

Your surroundings are more beautiful than before.

Your faith is deeper than before.

That—that right there—is resilience.

Verse for Thought

> "When you pass through the waters, I will be with you; and when you pass through the rivers, they will not sweep over you. When you walk through the fire, you will not be burned; the flames will not set you ablaze." (Isaiah 43:2 NIV)

Reflection Question

I was once taught this psychological party game where you ask people the following ice-breaker questions. Go ahead and answer them for yourself.

What is your favorite color? Why?

What is your favorite animal? Why?

Where is your favorite place in nature? Why?

Supposedly, your answers reveal the following:

1. Your favorite color will reveal how you feel about yourself.
2. Your favorite animal will reveal how you feel about your significant other or what you are looking for in a significant other.
3. Your favorite place in nature will reveal how you feel about God.

Did your answers to these questions reveal those truths? Why do you think this works?

Let Us Pray

> *How amazing Your creation is, oh God!*
> *Mighty is Your handiwork and Your love for me.*
> *Lord, I trust You and believe in Your promises for me.*
> *You delivered Noah through the flood;*
> *You delivered Shadrach, Meshach, and Abednego through the fire;*
> *and I believe that You will deliver me through the storms of this life.*
> *How glorious You are, God.*

*** By the grace and mighty power of God, my stepdad miraculously defied his 40 percent chance of survival diagnosis and made a full recovery.

20

The Resilience Collective

When you meet someone new, how do you introduce yourself? I have found that among young adults, the ice-breaker question that typically follows the name exchange is, "Are you in school, or do you work?" I used to characterize myself solely by my occupation. But despite my stubborn attitude and my first book title proposal (*Why I Dropped Out of College*), I have recently rededicated myself to finishing my degree.

The school that I attend is built on a hill. Of course, all of my classes are located at the very top of this hill, and each day this asthmatic huffs and puffs her way up the hill to the health-science building. Now, next to the health-science building is a tiny little snack shack, and this tiny little snack shack is known for having the best Chinese food in the world. In the four years that I have been attending this school, I have been too afraid to try this supposed best Chinese food in the world because at any given time there are at least thirty people in line. I seriously don't understand how this works—like where are they cooking this Chinese food, and how do they have enough food in this tiny little snack shack to be able to sustain all the people who are in line all day? When I walk by, I can smell how amazing the food is, and I can see the look of happiness on the faces of the people who braved the line and are enjoying the reward for their toil. But I could not justify standing in that line.

It is a very real and prevalent topic on campus. In fact, it is another common ice-breaker question. After students say, "Hello, my name is …" they often follow with, "Hey, have you tried that Chinese food?" and there are only two different responses to that question. One is "Yes! And now I am an advocate for that Chinese food. I am a believer. It is the best Chinese food in the world!" The second response is "Naw, dog. Have you *seen* that line? Ain't nobody got time for that!"

One day, a girl in one of my classes saw me eyeing her Chinese food. She offered to let me try some. I politely declined, but when she insisted that I try it, I gave in. And, boy, was that day a game changer. Now I am an advocate for that Chinese food. I am a believer. It is the best Chinese food in the world! The next day, I went to brave the line to get some of my very own best Chinese food in the world, and that same girl happened to be near the front of the line of thirty people. She beckoned me over and told me that she had a feeling that I would be there, so she had saved me a spot.

What if that was our attitude about faith? What if we did not allow ourselves to simply just ask people about Jesus? Because usually there are only two responses to "Do you know Jesus?" One is "Yes, I know Jesus! I am an advocate for Jesus. I am a believer. He is the best Savior in the world!" The second response is "Nah, dog. Religion isn't for me. Church is boring. Those perfect Christians are all hypocrites."

So what if we took it one step further? What if we actually went out and shared with others the goodness of God? The Bible literally commands that we "taste and see that the Lord is good" (Psalm 34:8a NIV). So let us be the ones who show up, lean in, and soak it all up. Then let us become the ones who go out and share Jesus with others. If Jesus did not come to earth to be served, but to serve, then why should we not do the same? (see Matthew 20:28). It is not our jobs to fluff up the message, because once others experience the power of the gospel for themselves, it is going to be a game changer for them. What we *can* do is act as vessels of grace.

We can show people who God is and what He does—whether that be by singing or studying or programming or building or teaching—and then we can prepare and save a spot for people at church. We can let them know that they belong there, that they are welcome, and that they are loved.

I am not perfect. Though I long to be, I never will be. My life is messy because of things done to me and because of things that I have done. And that's okay. God does not want our perfection anyway. He wants our attention. "My name is Jealous, and I am a jealous God," He told Moses (Exodus 34:14b The Voice). In fact, God does not want us to focus on perfection at all. He does not require that we constantly bring our sins to a confessional; instead, He merely asks that we surrender and staple our sins to the cross. He does not require that we pay for the penance ourselves; instead, He already paid for them through Jesus's death. Our sins do not have to disappoint God, because Jesus makes them dissipate until they disappear. He turns our messes into messages.

It is not called the *Holy* Bible because of the humans who penned the words. It is called the Holy Bible because of the dissertation of the gospel. Basically, the entire Bible is made up of messy mistakes. God loves using imperfection, because He just uses them to prove that failure is never final and is never fatal when He's involved. If you look at the genealogy of Jesus, it is filled with outcasts, outsiders, and the scandalous. Jesus's family reflects the one that He came to save. I love the way that the apostle Paul told his testimony: "Here's a word you can take to heart and depend on: Jesus Christ came into the world to save sinners. I'm proof—Public Sinner Number One—of someone who could never have made it apart from sheer mercy. And now he shows me off—evidence of his endless patience—to those who are right on the edge of trusting him forever" (1 Timothy 1:15–16 MSG).

Jesus came for those who feel lost and alone trying to make it through this world on their own.

He came for Noah, who was the only one in his small group.

He came for Moses, who slaughtered and stuttered.

He came for David, who slept around.

He came for the barren Elizabeth, who thought she was not getting what she asked for.

He came for the Virgin Mary, who thought she was getting what she did not ask for.

He came for you, friend.

Amid the mistakes, the despair, the destruction, and the distractions, God is always with us. He never abandons us; He delivers us through our adversities and then He advances our understandings and our abilities. Just look at the testimonies of faith that the ones before us left behind.

In faith, Noah continued the human race.

In faith, Moses led an entire nation out of bondage.

In faith, David defeated a giant.

In faith, Elizabeth gave birth even in her old age.

In faith, Mary gave birth to the Son of God.

The legend Billy Graham said, "From one end of the Bible to the other, God assures us that He will never go back on His promises." Wow. Not once does God say, "Figure it out yourself," "Dwell in worry," Or "Survive through your stress." No! Instead, He said over and over again "Trust in Me." Listen to this precious promise:

> "If you'll hold on to me for dear life," says God,
>> "I'll get you out of any trouble.
>> I'll give you the best of care if you'll only get to know and trust me.
>> Call me and I'll answer, be at your side in bad times;
>> I'll rescue you, then throw you a party.
>> I'll give you a long life, give you a long drink of salvation!" (Psalm 91:14–16 MSG)

I believe that God is going to do mighty things through you, friend. He can restore what is broken and turn it into something beautiful. Just have faith. When you strive to do things on your own, you are going to lose your confidence. But when you strive to do things through Christ, you are going to lose your insecurity.

With God, you can boldly declare:

Hello, my name is Resilient.

Verses for Thought

"You're blessed when you're at the end of your rope. With less of you there is more of God and his rule.

You're blessed when you feel you've lost what is most dear to you. Only then can you be embraced by the One most dear to you.

You're blessed when you're content with just who you are—no more, no less. That's the moment you find yourselves proud owners of everything that can't be bought.

You're blessed when you've worked up a good appetite for God. He's food and drink in the best meal you'll ever eat.

You're blessed when you care. At the moment of being 'care-full,' you find yourselves cared for.

You're blessed when you get your inside world—your mind and heart—put right. Then you can see God in the outside world.

You're blessed when you can show people how to cooperate instead of compete or fight. That's when you discover who you really are, and your place in God's family.

You're blessed when your commitment to God provokes persecution. The persecution drives you even deeper into God's kingdom.

Not only that—count yourselves blessed every time people put you down or throw you out or speak lies about you to discredit me. What it means is that the truth is too close for comfort and they are uncomfortable. You can be glad when that happens—give a cheer, even!—for though they don't like it, *I* do! And all heaven applauds.

And know that you are in good company. My prophets and witnesses have always gotten into this kind of trouble." (Matthew 5:3–12 MSG)

Reflection Question

What is your story?

Let Us Pray

God, You are so good.
I know that You have a purpose for me.
I will trust in You always.
You are the only reason that I've made it this far.
I can't go a day without You.
Help me be a light for You all the days of my life.
I love You.
Amen.

Epilogue

It was my dream to see the Mona Lisa. So during our Europe trip last summer, my brother and I purchased a plane ticket, a train pass, and booked an appointment at the Louvre. When we arrived at the giant museum, my brother and I spent hours maneuvering our way through the labyrinth of rooms filled with art and artifacts. Some rooms were really cool, and some rooms really sucked (I mean, how many naked statues do you really need?). Eventually, I became bored and tired of aimlessly searching, and I settled to take a picture with a picture of the Mona Lisa. That was when I saw the real her through a break in the crowds: the masterpiece that I had been searching for all along.

This is similar to how I have been living life up until the release of this book. I have spent years wandering, lost, and frustrated as to why God would allow me to search through so many dead ends; but I have realized that my purpose is not found in my career, my title, or my status. My purpose is found through the journey of holding God's hand through the museum of life, admiring the good parts and laughing at the bad while inviting people to join us along the way.

I like to think that God and I have an ironic, hilarious relationship. Over the course of my wanderings through the museum of life, I have noticed myself often retreat and circle back to certain safety rooms. In moments of bravery, I meander into new rooms just to "try things out," but then I run back to my comfort zone. There were certain rooms that I had roped off as areas that "I hated" (such as cats and children), but really I was just too afraid to recognize God's calling on my heart towards such things.

Since completing this book, I have finally begun a career of teaching preschool. Yes, this is as ironic as it gets, people. But I enjoy it. I still travel in the off season, and I am studying to get a degree in Theology. I don't know where else I am going from here, but I am prepared to continue this crazy adventure hand-in-hand with my God.

After all, if there was a straight, empty hallway that led straight through to the Mona Lisa, what fun would that have been?

Acknowledgments

Thank you ...

- to my Lord Jesus Christ, the author and perfecter of my faith, my life, and this book.
- to Ivy, the original, one-and-only audience of *Story Time with Jess!* at the bus stop. Thank you for listening and laughing.
- to Olivia, for telling me to write this book in the first place.
- to Ryan, for inspiring me to experiment and try new things with my writing layout.
- to Morghan, for being there no matter what with a listening heart and an encouraging spirit.
- to my SB family, particularly John, Christian, and Eddie, for always asking how the writing is going.
- to Bus Ben, for being so kind, caring, and honest.
- to my Hillsong family, for all of your excitement, love, and support.
- to Fonz, for always having my back.

And thank you to my generous and loving family
for your patience and encouragement.

Printed in the United States
By Bookmasters